"One of the best elements of the book is the writing style. It is written in such a manner that you might imagine Faith is sitting across from you and telling you her life story over a cup of tea." — Jennifer Donovan, professional book reviewer, Phenix City, Alabama

"...Organized thoughtfully and chronologically.. [that] enhanced the flow, and... kept me glued from its beginning until the end." — Fazzier, Online Book Club reviewer

"With the coronavirus pandemic we're dealing with today, Faith's message seems timely, relevant, and important." —Edwin L. Lamont, DTM, President, Bill Gove Golden Gavel Toastmasters Club, Boynton Beach, Florida

"A perfect blend of a riveting inspirational story and practical advice to help you live more positively, happier, healthier, and longer."— David J. Pollay, bestselling author of *The Law of the Garbage Truck* and *The 3 Promises*

"This book would be a fantastic read for someone who lives with a disability or has a child with a disability, and it would also be greatly enjoyed by those who are inspired by resiliency." — Jennifer Donovan, professional book reviewer, Phenix City, Alabama

"... (Faith's) triumphs were the most inspiring... They left me energized and motivated me to overcome my own life challenges and live a fuller life." — Fazzier, Online Book Club reviewer

Blind BLACK SHEEP

An Extraordinary Story of Defiance, Persistence, and Faith

DICK ROBINSON and FAITH BLOCK

Legacy Scribe Books

Blind Black Sheep: An Extraordinary Story of Defiance, Persistence, and Faith

Autobiography | Physical Impairments | Dysfunctional Families | Inspirational and Personal Growth

Library of Congress Control Number: 2019916623
ISBN: 978-0-578-59429-3 (Paperback)
ISBN: 978-0-578-59496-5 (eBook)

All events in the book are true, based on the subject's best memories, and are not intended to harm anyone.

Printed in the USA
First printing edition 2020

Publisher
Legacy Scribe Books, LLC
10139 44th Terrace South, #373
Boynton Beach, FL 33436
legacyscribe.com
blindblacksheep.com

For Naomi, Amanda, Kaylee, and Chloe

"Have faith . . . things will be better tomorrow."

CONTENTS

ACKNOWLEDGMENTS

We want to thank our awesome editor, Brenda Moore Robinson, Dick's wife. She corrected the drafts, made the photo collages, and served as our visual advisor. We did nothing visually, including the book covers, without her approval. Thank you so much, Brenda.

Our book cover designer, Donna Cunningham of BeauxArts.Design, had brilliant ideas and executed them perfectly, even while most people slept. We're perfectionists, and Donna did everything to make us look good.

Elsie Jaehn put some final proofreading touches on the book shortly before it was published. We kept telling her, "Hey, Elsie, that was a good catch." She was a valuable member of the team.

Lastly, we want to thank family and friends who supported our work. That includes Amanda Karchmer, Faith's granddaughter, who captured her grandma's happiness in the photo on the back cover.

FOREWORD

Blind Black Sheep is a deeply personal story of one extraordinary person's life. I read this entire book in one sitting, eager to know what happened next. It entertains, enlightens, and imparts practical life lessons that can help anyone with the desire to live more positively and authentically. This memoir is an uplifting example of how positivity can overcome any challenge in life. Despite being an outcast, Faith Block found joy doing what she loved and helping others. You are capable of finding happiness if you put in time and energy.

Her message: "Don't let disabilities or challenges stop you from being happy and enjoying every minute of the day." This theme is significant and timely. Everyone needs a good dose of inspiration to get us through periods of high stress. I can't think of anyone more credible to have written this type of book. It's really the story of you, complete with specific life lessons that can have a profound and resounding impact on your life. *Blind Black Sheep* tells a compelling, candid story that will stay with you long after you finish the last page.

Enjoy,

Courtney E. Ackerman

April 23, 2020

(Courtney E. Ackerman is a positive psychologist and a researcher with one of California's health and human services agencies. She is the author of four inspirational books: *My Pocket Meditations for Self-Compassion, My Pocket Gratitude, 5-Minute Bliss,* and *My Pocket Positivity.* She is a regular contributor to positivepsychology.com and has been published in the *International Journal of Wellbeing.*)

INTRODUCTION

Why should you care about me and my scandalous story? I'm an active 92-year-old mother, grandma, and former elementary school teacher and professional counselor to the elderly. I've made the world a better place. I'm a good person—giving to the needy, praying for people, apologizing for mistakes, listening to stories, and hugging people with love.

My story is an uplifting, personal journey of overcoming blindness (Part One), a dysfunctional family (Part Two), and my own character flaws and rebirth (Part Three), followed by Life Lessons (Part Four). This autobiography is entirely true, based on my best memory of actual events and conversations as they happened or likely happened. I did not write it to hurt anyone.

I was fortunate to meet professional writer and historian Dick Robinson. We put together this book. I first thought it would just be an ordinary coffee-table book for my living room. But it was destined for wider distribution. You rarely find an autobiography that specifically teaches you how to change your life forever. I promise you'll discover insight, inspiration, and life lessons to help you become a better person.

Faithfully yours,

Faith Block

Boynton Beach, Florida
April 16, 2020

1

PART 1:
SOMETHING'S VERY WRONG
(1927-1939)

[Page Intentionally Blank]

FAMILY PHOTOS

As a toddler with my doll Polly

Leander Stone School Grade 7 or 8. I'm back row, 2nd from left; best friend Esther is 3rd from left.

Mr. & Mrs. George Block

College days

George & me

Mom & Morley

Me, my mom, baby Naomi

Dad & Fran

Dad & Shelly

FAMILY PHOTOS

George & me

Council for the Jewish Elderly Adult Day Care Center where I worked in programming and volunteers for 25 years. I am in pink at left.

I caught the biggest fish!

Kaylee, Naomi, Eric, Amanda, Chloe

Purple Hair Vegas 2018
Naomi, Amanda and me

CHAPTER 1:
Pennies on the Floor

High above the heart of downtown Chicago, renowned eye doctor Harry Gradle shocked Mom and me: "Faith should learn to read Braille." Mom, an eternal optimist, barked back, "No, I won't have that. She's only eight, and we're not going to have her give up playing with her friends. She'll learn typing instead." I agreed with Mom. It was the one moment in my ninety-two years that changed my life forever.

I refused to learn Braille, the writing system for the blind with raised dot letters. If people thought I was blind, they might disapprove of me, belittle me, and avoid me. Society then thought "blind people were miserable creatures incapable of advancement and self-enrichment," according to Helen Keller.

Legally blind, I had my whole life ahead of me. I just wanted to be healthy, loved, and given a chance to develop my full potential myself. If I was stigmatized as blind, I might never find my actual ability as a person, able to do anything I really desired in life. Against all the odds, I desperately battled a vision monster inside of me in strange worlds. I discovered how to change my life at home, but I paid a whopping price.

At the start of the Great Depression on Chicago's South Side, I bonded with Mom in the kitchen and fought with her in the living room. Mom enjoyed baking and did a lot of it. She was a fabulous baker, and I relished being in the kitchen with her. She always made me part of what she was cooking.

When I was just three, Mom gave me some dough, and I played with it. I blackened my pie dough by dropping it on the floor and smooshing it on other dirty surfaces. Mom put her hands on mine and guided my dirty fingers, shaping the dough into a crust. Mom said, "Give me your dough, and I'll cook it in the oven with my apple pie." I gave Mom absolutely black dough. Mom always stated, "Oh, this is gonna make a pretty little apple pie."

Sixty minutes later, Mom pulled both our pies out of the oven, with golden brown crusts and aroma that filled my home. I was so proud I made a cute little pie for me. And it was as good as Mom's! Sweet Mom didn't tell me that she threw out my dough, and, while I wasn't looking, she baked a small pie for me.

But in the living room, Mom wasn't so friendly. She was strict. She shaped me into a typical kid. One day before lunch, Mom surprised me with a game she created, called Find the Pennies. I enjoyed playing parlor games, liked Simon Says. But the start of this game scared me.

She'd fling a fist-full of pennies on the living room floor of our small, sparsely furnished, fifty-five-dollars-a-month apartment in Chicago's largest and oldest black neighborhood, named Bronzeville. Some eighty copper pennies ricocheted and scattered everywhere off the variegated copper-colored oak wood floor. The pennies echoed thunderously in the spacious bare room, BRA-TA-TAT, like a magazine of heavy .45-caliber bullets from a machine gun of my South Side neighbor Al Capone. After that fearful barrage, Mom ordered, "Now, Faith, find all those pennies. This will help improve your eyes." That was my first vivid memory.

I could barely see less than a foot in front of me clearly. Everything else was blurry. I'd crawl on my hands and floor-burned knees in a white, frilly dress hunting pennies for thirty or forty-five minutes. I became exhausted and frustrated. I couldn't see the pennies. They blended into the color of the floor.

I stopped looking for the pennies. I got up, crying, "Mommy, I can't find any more pennies." I threw up my hands in an "I give up" gesture. I pleaded, "Can I please stop?" She replied sternly, yet supportively, "No, you have to find all of them. You can find them all. There's only two or three more." Mom wouldn't ever let me quit, even if I found all the pennies, except for just a couple. Sometimes she'd help me a little – "There are three more. Find them!" She often reminded me: "It's not punishment, Faith. It will help you later."

Nothing usually stopped me. I made up my mind, I would find every penny, no matter how long it took. And eventually, I did! I found more than 54,000 pennies playing Mom's game over those few years. Ironically, I learned today that Braille pupils develop finger strength and grip by finding and counting pennies hidden in Play-Doh.

At home, I was an innocent, naive child with a heart of gold—well, maybe copper pennies, anyway. But outside, I was not so pure. I became a cocky, six-year-old tomboy. We moved to Drumheller, Canada, with my normalcy needs escalating. At the start of the Depression, this one-street coal-mining town in the badlands of Alberta attracted farmers and dozens of Jews. They escaped Russian pogroms, the massacre of Jews, for vast tracts of cheap land.

Despite my blindness, I was the only girl who played with older ruffian boys, including my older brother Morley and Cousin Jerry.

Mom never accepted me as a tomboy and dressed me in girly dresses. Even as a third-grader, I was "motivationally gifted"—not allowing my handicap to hold me back. Compared to healthy kids, I could hardly see. I could make out distant shapes and colors.

Chapter 1 Pennies on the Floor

Yet, I was having the time of my life. Mom taught me, "Disability does not stop you from enjoying life every minute of every day."

I was unstoppable, I thought. I did things only my way. Even though I was reckless, I didn't play on or near the railroad tracks. A couple boys were killed on the tracks. I was terrified of those rails.

I found "low hanging forbidden fruit," though. That was sliding down Aunt Gertie and Uncle Jack's long banister. They had a big house in Drumheller. Jerry would say, "Hey, the coast is clear. Let's go for it now." We slid down—what seemed like a forty-foot dark mahogany banister—giggling all the way. We often got caught. But that didn't stop us. We did it repeatedly for the thrill of getting away with something. Life, though, wasn't always fun and games for me.

Mom and Dad were once a happily married young couple with a toddler son and a new "adorable" baby on the way (me). Dad (Joe) was a hard-working plumbing supplies salesman who searched for a niche in business. Dear Mom (Bessie) was a traditional housewife who kept the household together. She kept busy keeping a kosher kitchen, cleaning the house, and raising Morley, three, the cutest tot you've ever seen.

They were the perfect All-American, working-class family. Mom and Dad coveted a happy, close family of two or three children. When she was pregnant with me, my whole family enjoyed communal energy. We had a large family. It included my mom and her parents and six siblings, and Dad and his mom and four siblings plus cousins. I would be born into a comfort zone of family and friends.

In Mom's womb, my oxygen supply was running out. I couldn't breathe. Suddenly, I felt liquid rushing past me, pushing me into a narrow tunnel. I was in pain. I felt lots of pressure on me, and it seemed to last forever. I was desperately running out of oxygen and fighting fatigue.

A cold, bright light and dry air hit my body like a brick wall. It was a surprise. I felt like yelping but couldn't. I could only tell the difference between lightness and darkness. I heard loud sounds I've never heard before. I twisted my body ninety degrees in the tight channel. I positioned my little hands, pulled my naked body free, and landed in a new, odd place.

As I gasped for oxygen, I let out a penetrating wail. I was born! I felt like crying. So I did. I didn't hold anything back. It felt good. I was already unique. I developed my one-of-a-kind fingerprints in Mom's womb just by touching the surroundings. Soon, Mom's angelic voice that I recognized from the womb spoke to me. Another voice whispered in my ear. I didn't know what those sounds meant. But they were music to my ears.

Chapter 1 Pennies on the Floor

Only minutes old, I was in a puzzling new place that I never experienced before. I was warm in the womb. But now the air felt cold. Someone was holding me. Their arms were warm—and that made me feel secure. I saw some light through my brand-new eyes. But I really couldn't see anything else, even shapes. I was drooling.

I flashed my first smile, a reflex smile, not in response to anything. I was testing my equipment. After waiting for months, my parents and brother finally met me. As I moved, they admired all my flawless little features and gushed, "So cute."

I stretched and yawned. Morley uttered, "Awww." He thought I was the most loveable baby he'd ever seen.

I kicked my legs freely in the air in a wiggly motion. My legs felt no resistance that I experienced cramped up in the womb. I felt tremendous relief. I wrapped my tiny fingers around someone's pinky and breathed softly on the back of their hand. Must have been Mom's. I smelled the same smell all around me that I did in the womb.

I heard voices nearby. I didn't know what was happening or even what to expect next. But I recognized Mom's voice that I had often heard in her womb. Dad uttered a sigh of relief. Dad, with glossy eyes, exclaimed to Mom, "Bessie, we have a beautiful, picture-perfect daughter. Just what we wanted." Mom didn't say anything and looked adoringly at me. Mom's exhaustion just melted away. She got out some beautiful thoughts: "Her eyes are sparkling, her little hands are so cute. She's lighter than I expected and smells divine. She looks so flawless to me."

Everyone in Chicago was celebrating my birth, of course, in 1927 during the giddy Roaring Twenties and Prohibition. Chicago then was booming with bootleg gin, jazz, and gangsters. Just a dizzy, silly time. People sat on flagpoles, swallowed live goldfish, and everyone danced the Charleston. America's most famous gangster Al Capone made my city notorious for violence.

People were never so prosperous. It was time to partay! It was my raucous coming-out party.

At Michael Reese Hospital, Mom and Dad's eyes sparkled, and both glowed with joyful tears. Dad, with raised, prominent cheekbones, asked, "What will we name her?" Then frowning said, "Oh, wait. Why isn't she looking at me? And what's that white stuff in her eyes?" He grabbed Mom's elbow, uttering, "Oh, my God! Something's terribly wrong." Dad wrinkled his brow, rushed out of the room, and returned with a doctor. The doctor, an intern, agreed that my eyes didn't look right.

Dad asked, "What's wrong, doc?" After taking a close look, the doctor replied, "She's got cataracts in both eyes, impairing her eyesight. It's unusual for a newborn to have cataracts. But you should have her looked at by an eye specialist." My parents, destitute immigrants of Russian heritage, were seeking "the American Dream." Mom and Dad wished I'd be successful and prosperous through hard work, determination, and initiative. And now they set aside their hopes and faced my calamity!

They sensed their lives being turned upside down. Mom and Dad glared at each other, even at hospital workers. They strongly felt many natural emotions under these circumstances—anger, resentment, and bitterness. And most of all—uncertainty. They feared that I wouldn't ever see them. Dad lamented as he glanced around the hospital nursery, "Everything was going so well. Why is this happening to us?"

Dad saw healthy-looking babies all around him. I might not have good vision like them. But it seemed that the world dangled normal vision in front of me and said, "Try to get it." My parents' big hope was that I'd be productive in school, at work, and in society. They were afraid I'd be hidden away like many disabled children in other countries then.

I was different from the second I was born. All babies are born legally blind, then sight develops quickly. My eyesight didn't improve. I had significant, cloudy cataracts and immature pupils in both eyes, blocking my view. There were only three babies like me with congenital cataracts of every 1,000 births. No one knows what caused my eye problems. But researchers say half of congenital cataracts are hereditary. My condition startled Mom and Dad. They thought only older people and aging pets got cataracts.

PART 1 SOMETHING'S VERY WRONG

At the hospital, Mom counted my fingers and toes, making sure they were all there. She gently brushed her fingers through patches of curly hair on my baldish head and connected with me. Mom says she named me after Aunt Faith. I didn't have an Aunt Faith. I never found out who this mystery person was. Faith was a rare name for 1927 but was becoming more popular. Faith means trust and confidence. It's a short and sweet name with a Catholic saint (Saint Faith) or spiritual connotation. My name had a foretelling meaning to me. I needed a lot of trust, faith, and spirituality in controlling my destiny.

When I was a few days old, Mom held me tightly against her breast and grinned at me. But I couldn't see her. Mom smiled widely, looking desperately for one of those big smiling-happy-baby responses. Those real smiles, though, usually don't come for several weeks. I didn't know whether I ever could give Mom those joyous, precious love signals. I felt sorry for her. I missed out on those bonding moments and couldn't grow our loving relationship. I felt helpless like many blind people first do. Later, I'd have learning problems with crawling, walking, playing, talking, reading, writing, and making friends.

I couldn't see with my eyes. But I "saw" with my senses—touch, hearing, and smell. As mother cuddled me against her chest, she touched my little hand, and instinctively, I grasped her pinky finger. I was surprised we were already communicating. Her touch was saying, "I love you," and I guess my contact was saying, "I love you too, Mom."

Eyes are the most important sensory organ. More than 80 percent of what normal children process comes through their eyes, according to researchers. For me, I took in mostly through hearing (11 percent in healthy children) and much less by smell, touch, and taste.

Over the next month, when I heard Mom near me, I let out a big "Wahhhhh wah wah!" This signaled Mom that I was hungry, cold, or wet. A healthy baby may see her caregiver close by and often cries.

Many family members and their friends visited me. They didn't know I had limited vision. Visitors smiled, made wide-eyed babyfaces, and talked to me in silly baby voices. They said "Hi" to me. But I'd thought to myself, "Who are these people with silly baby voices?" Relatives would look at me and say, "Why isn't she paying attention to me when I talk to her?" Many developmental milestones, like smiling, happen much later in babies with visual impairments.

From birth, my outlook was bleak. My eyes didn't talk to my brain, letting me know what I saw. My mind was degenerating. Yet, my parents didn't accept that I was imperfect. They thought I'd someday soon be healthy and happy as most people were in the 1920s. Mom and Dad still looked forward to a bright life ahead. And they wouldn't let me shatter their American Dream.

[Page Intentionally Blank]

CHAPTER 2:
Like Father, Like Daughter

I t's not common to hear the phrase, "Like father, like daughter." It's not an everyday expression as, "Like father, like son." That expression comes from traditional gender roles of sons acting like their dads or following in their footsteps. Dads traditionally made sure daughters married well.

But in today's more modern world, a father usually passes his tendencies or life's work to a daughter. In my family, I was a lot like my father, especially his bullheadedness and ambitions.

Dad had a powerful impact on my entire life. That's why I talk so much about him in this book. He's affected all my relationships from birth until today and will until my death. That includes relationships I've had with family and friends. My early interactions with my father set self-esteem and social patterns projected into all my relationships. A dad's role in the way their child grows and develops is often overshadowed by a mom's role in our society. New evidence shows that supportive fathers have children who develop better social skills and language.

Children of non-supportive dads with emotional disorders from their own childhood often have more behavioral and emotional difficulties. This is why I think Dad's childhood and youth affected my life, especially in adolescence. His harsh life in the old country created some flaws in my childhood behavior. Dad's willpower was in me—and it was devastating in school and at home.

As a six-year-old first-grader in Drumheller, I was a good student. I got pleasure from reading. I had to hold material close to my eyes. The Dick and Jane and other books all had print big enough so I could easily understand them.

But I did stupid things that made me seem disobedient. My teacher, Mrs. McKensie, brought out a manual pencil sharpener one day. I had never seen a pencil sharpener before. I purposely broke my pencil point lead and went and sharpened my pencil. I loved winding the sharpener handle and seeing the peeled wood coming off the pencil. That fascinated me.

About fifteen minutes later, during quiet time, I purposely smashed my pencil lead for the second time and sharpened my pencil again. I wound the handle slowly so I could watch the peeling spiral out of the machine longer. That was so much fun. Then I took my seat. Another fifteen or thirty minutes later, I purposely broke my pencil again for the third time and sharpened it. The students, especially the teacher, watched my every move.

I returned to my seat, and Mrs. McKensie earnestly advised me, "Faith, stop breaking your pencil on purpose and sharpening it." Of course, I didn't mind my teacher. I usually did what I wanted to do. So, a little while later, I broke my shortened pencil for the fourth time and headed towards the pencil sharpener.

Deepening her tone, my teacher ordered me: "Faith, go to your seat." Obediently, I rushed to my desk. I was shaking, sheepishly quivering. The teacher ordered me firmly, "Fold your hands." I thought I was getting a "time-out." I folded my hands, interlocking my fingers like I was praying.

Instead of ordering me to a time-out, she got something from her desk. I didn't see what it was at first. But then as she got closer, I saw it was about a two-foot black leather strap, like a belt. Fearing for the worst, I closed my eyes. Then, whack, whack, whack. She flogged my knuckles hard three times and scolded me, "Don't ever do that again!"

I can still feel that strap's sharp sting some eighty-five years later, and the sudden embarrassment as my fellow pupils watched in shock. Luckily, my hands didn't bleed. But my knuckles were red, and my face was crimson. I just felt like hiding under my seat but didn't. You could hear a pin drop. My classmates sat still in their seats and didn't dare say a thing.

I never saw Mrs. McKensie punish other pupils like that. She wasn't mean, just extremely unyielding. And I can't blame her. She was right, and I was wrong. The rules were the rules. When you're reading, you're supposed to read, and when you're supposed to be writing, you write. And when you're not supposed to go to the pencil sharpener, you don't go there!

On the way home from school that day, Jerry, who saw my thrashing, didn't make me feel any better. Jerry rubbed it in, "You should have known better. You were told not to do it." I just cringed. I didn't say a word. But I could feel that crimson flush creeping across my cheeks again.

Today, I chuckle about that incident. I put all the blame on me. I did not obey my teacher. Everybody minded the teacher . . . but obstinate me!

I didn't always mind Mom, either. Sometimes you couldn't reason with me. At Christmas one of my gifts was a pair of brown leather dress gloves—just thin pigskin. I had mittens. I was so excited about the gloves, I insisted, "Mom, I'm going to wear them to school and show all my friends." My mother cautioned, "No, you'll freeze your hands. There's no lining in them." I didn't care what Mom thought. I wore the gloves proudly walking to school a couple blocks away. Her last words to me as I left the house were, "You'll be sorry!" Mother was always right!

CHAPTER 2 Like Father, Like Daughter

It was a bitterly cold, three degrees Fahrenheit, snowy January day in Drumheller, just north of the Montana state line. By the time I walked a few blocks and pulled open the schoolhouse door, I couldn't feel anything in my hands. I removed my gloves. Both hands were red, tingling, and frozen solid.

Jerry and a few other kids from the first and second grades went out into the snow with a big basin, put snow in it, and brought it back inside. "Put your hands in here," Jerry said. I kept my hands in this freezing basin for a couple hours until my fingers thawed. I can't tell you how humiliating this was for me. I had terrible frostbite, which can lead to gangrene. Winters bothered my hands for many years.

Oh, my God, I can see my hands today in that white basin of snow, and Jerry calling me, "Stupid" for wearing thin dress gloves in that cold. If someone told me not to do something, I did it anyway. I was persistent. I had a high IQ, but sometimes I showed sheer stupidity.

At times, my inner demon was my reckless, lousy eyesight. As a child, I cherished playing at the playground for regular kids. I would never use a playground for children with disabilities. I thought I was an average kid. Dangerously running around the playground, not seeing clearly where I was going. Hanging from the monkey bars. Seeing who could swing the highest. "Hey, look at me," I hollered with a big grin that could not be contained. I was standing up on the swing seat, going higher than the other kids could.

My favorite was the swing. "How do you like to go up in a swing? Up in the air so blue?" I'd quote that from Robert Louis Stevenson's *The Swing* to friends. I didn't soar to the clouds, though.

Even with bad vision, I l-o-v-v-v-e-d running under occupied, high-flying swing seats. When a seated swinger was high up in the air at a peak, I'd run under the swing seat before it came back down. I was quite successful at my daredevil game until one day . . . my limited vision misjudged the timing. The swinger was going higher and higher by raising his legs at the top of each swing.

Mother yelled, "Faith, watch out!" Wham. The wooden swing seat hit me directly in my mouth with a massive force, knocking me to the ground. Mom rushed bleeding me in a cab to the hospital, where I had several stitches on both sides of my mouth. The tiny marks are still visible today. I don't know if the pain I felt was from the swing seat smashing my face or my indignation from doing this to myself. Anyway, Mom soothed the sting by feeding me chocolate malts and ice cream. Unlucky and lucky me.

Every time Esther, my best friend, and I went to the park, she'd say, "Let's run under the swings." She never got hurt, and she was the instigator. It was like the blind leading the blind, I joked. Her legally blind eyesight was worse than mine. I was a fearless little miss daredevil.

CHAPTER 2 Like Father, Like Daughter

Nothing prevents me from doing what I want to do when I want to do it. No matter what people will say or what happens to me. That's just the way I was, and I am. Even though I was hurt by a swing seat, I still ran around without regard for my safety.

In his Russian childhood, my father suffered hard times. That shaped his life in North America, and mine too. I was undoubtedly tenacious like him. I looked more like Mom, but I behaved more like Dad.

In the early 1900s, Dad's family suffered a tragedy in Russia. Dad was born in 1901 and raised in Berezovka, Ukraine. Berezovka, part of Russia, was in suburban Odessa, a major port on the Black Sea. His parents, Berezovka-born Moishe Brickman and Bessie Sheps, were raising five children, ages three to eleven. I don't know what work grandpa did. But I know most Jews there were small shop owners and craftsmen, living in the small farming community of rolling green hills with goats, tethered or roaming near their old homes.

At age ten, my father, Jacob Brickman (later changed to Joseph), became the family's father figure. He was named after his paternal grandfather, Yakov, a Russian or Hebrew variant of the given name Jacob. Dad was the oldest male of two boys and three girls in the close-knit family of Moishe and Bessie.

In 1911, Russians and anti-Semites killed Joe's father, Moishe, only forty-one, in Berezovka during the pogroms.

PART 1 SOMETHING'S VERY WRONG

They penalized Jews for taking part in the economic-political discontent during the 1905 Russian Revolution against the Russian Empire. Berezovka was a heavily Jewish city caught up in the pogroms and the ensuing Nazi-atrocity Holocaust. Anti-Semitic crimes in Europe claimed the lives of six million other Jews in the Holocaust in the first half of the 1900s.

Grandma Bessie (Basyia in Russia), only age thirty, and her young children were left with little or no money. Grandma opened a restaurant-bar in Berezovka, hoping it would help feed the kids. Dad and big sister Gertie (Gela), eleven, filled beer bottles in the tavern basement for sale in the bar.

Bessie struggled running the bar and bringing up her youngest of five children. They were: Anne (Anna, as listed in a government document), three; Nettie (Richane), six; and Louis (Leba), eight. After a brief time, Bessie knew the tavern couldn't support them. Disappointed and frustrated, she closed the bar and planned a new course of action.

In the early 1900s, many Jewish shop owners and craftsmen were fleeing Berezovka for new lives in North America, either the U.S. or Canada. While she was running the bar, Bessie was thinking about it too. There was only one problem. She was broke. How would she pay for her 4,700-mile trip to the "land of opportunity"?

CHAPTER 2 Like Father, Like Daughter

The family may have moved from Berezovka to the City of Odessa and lived with Bessie's brother-in-law Herschel Brickman. Bessie's brother Benny Sheps (my great-uncle) of Winnipeg, Manitoba, Canada, paid for the trip to America. An adult third-class ticket on a steamer then cost about thirty-five dollars, which would be about 962 dollars today. It was not cheap. But Benny could afford it.

In December 1913, Joe and his impoverished family left Russian-controlled Ukraine for America on the way to Winnipeg. They dreamed of a thriving good, new life in North America, where they could find jobs and freedom. They needed to escape the memories of famine, disease, dire poverty, and religious persecution of Russian Jews. Most of all, they needed to move beyond the horrible death of Moishe.

Many immigrants had unrealistically lofty expectations of life in America. It was not as one young man enthused, "America is all puddings and pies!" Joe and his family would soon find that out.

Bessie took her five young kids on a train and boat from Odessa to Liverpool, England, and across the Atlantic for nine days to Portland, Maine. Bessie's brother Benny paid for the trip.

But they suffered the worst fate of all: unbelievably being sent back to Liverpool—another nine days at sea. Immigration officers insisted they couldn't stay in America. Louis developed a contagious eye infection called

27

conjunctivitis or pinkeye. Freedom in America was ripped out right from under them.

Bessie was as furious as a monstrous storm on the treacherous sea. Known as "The General" in the family, she was rigid, harsh, and now livid. Louis was bothered by itchy, watery eyes and a "sleep" discharge for most of the voyage. He was contagious for several days to several weeks, caused by a virus or bacteria he may have picked up on a contaminated towel or something on the unsanitary ship. Uniformed federal officers, watching for cholera outbreaks, quarantined Louis for the return trip. This was one disease—and memory—the family could not escape.

Two months later, the Brickmans boarded the steamship S.S. Merion of the American Line and sailed for two weeks to Philadelphia. Again, on Benny's dime. I don't know how grandma managed a second-long ocean voyage with two young teens and three children between six and ten. The kids were bored, invented games to pass the time, and sometimes got into fights.

The family played some games on deck, but often faced foul-tasting food, cramped sleeping quarters and illnesses (typhus, cholera, and dysentery) that spread like epidemics. They met extremely crowded conditions all over the ship. The Merion held 1,800 passengers. It was the height of immigration from southern and eastern Europe—twenty-five million immigrants over the last fifty years.

CHAPTER 2 Like Father, Like Daughter

As they gleefully left the ship, tears welled up behind the eyelids of Bessie, Joe, and Gertie. They wiped away the tears, then their eyes went heavenward. Bessie let out a huge breath. She was relieved that this time the family could stay.

Upon arrival, Dad saw bananas for the first time in his life. He devoured a bunch of them from a wagon of golden bananas usually found along the docks. Uh-oh. He got sick to his stomach. The story goes that he never ate a banana or anything made with bananas for the rest of his life. So much for Philadelphia, the City of Brotherly Love!

Dad's immediate family got out of Europe just in time. They arrived in Philadelphia in February of 1914. That was five months before the start of World War I and before the 1917 Russian Revolution. During the revolution, Bolshevik leader Vladimir Lenin seized power and later set up the world's first communist state.

Had they not left then, I don't know if they would ever have gotten out of Russia—or if I would ever have been born. They were in the last big wave of Russian immigrants fleeing to America before the war.

After Dad recovered from eating too many bananas, the family took a train from Philadelphia via Chicago to Winnipeg on the Western Canadian prairies. Winnipeg, eh? Winnipeg, the capital of Manitoba province, is sixty-two miles just north of the Minnesota border. Winnipeg was once a fur trading post. When Joe lived there in the

1920s, the city boomed with the arrival of the railways and a flood of immigrants.

Grandma Bessie entered Canada with three hundred dollars in her purse, probably spending money from her brothers. That would be like having $7,200 in your purse today. Quite a stash. Bessie and her five children lived with or near her brothers, in Winnipeg. Finally, the family settled into a new home, a grueling two months after they left Berezovka.

Just age thirteen, Dad was recovering from the stress of the brutal trip. He was now facing the frightening pressure of supporting his family. When Dad arrived, Winnipeg, like most places, was in an economic depression with high unemployment. Still, many immigrants came in droves. Their hopes were dashed by the start of World War I. Families fought for money and food. Men left for the battlefields, thousands never returned or came home permanently disabled.

But the Brickmans were safe on the Western Canadian plains. All they knew was that war broke out between rival European countries. What mattered to them was having a roof over their heads, food on the table, and getting some pocket money.

The Brickmans were penniless during a Winnipeg depression that stopped the city's meteoric rise in Canadian manufacturing. They lived with Benny for a while until they could find work. The Sheps brothers, Benny and

CHAPTER 2 Like Father, Like Daughter

George, had recently started their own business. They ran Sheps Agencies Ltd., which became a large company in real estate, insurance, and managing apartment buildings. Other Winnipeg aunts and uncles helped support Dad's family for several months until they found a home near Benny.

Against all the odds, finally, Dad, fourteen, got a job as a hardware store helper, which paid him little or no money. But Dad did it for the family. He put them first. Under high stress, he was given more family responsibility than expected for a teenager. Older sis Gertie, sixteen, became a garment worker during tough union salary bargaining and strikes. Dad and Gertie were child laborers and became part of the working class. They were gaining in their fight for food, clothing, and shelter. Were they on the road to financial security?

Joe dreamed about what many young boys do. He thought about leaving home and doing something bigger in life. Much bigger than just a hardware store helper who stocked shelves and swept the floor. He visualized fighting in World War I in the Canadian Army against German troops. Canada then was part of the British Empire that declared war on Germany. The uniform might have lured Dad, displaying callous militarized masculinity. He might have been unhappy at home and hated his hardware store job.

Indeed, a private's pay of one dollar and ten cents a day was more than he got at the hardware store. The Army paid the going rate for men who were unskilled laborers. Three regular Army meals a day would be better than he was getting at home. Dad was ambitious and sought after more in life. Unfortunately, the Army rejected him. He was too young. Dad was sixteen, and the minimum age was eighteen. Dad's self-esteem plummeted. Feeling numb, he vowed never to be denied like this again.

During the war, young Joe wasn't ready to support his family yet. But he may have learned something important in Winnipeg. Dad unconsciously discovered a lesson in his teens that shaped his career decades later. Before he arrived in Winnipeg, the Canadian government recruited hearty fellow Ukrainians to the plains of Western Canada. They brought in people from rural farm communities with harsh climates, like Berezovka. Some 170,000 Europeans flocked to Winnipeg and Western Canada around the turn of the century.

The government thought they'd make good, rugged farmers. But they didn't. Numerous rural settlements failed as a result. Most recruited Jews weren't sturdy farmers. Many Jews left in outlying areas then settled in the city of Winnipeg in the early 1900s and became successful business people. The lesson: Most Jews make better business people than farmers. Dad followed this business model. As a teen, he didn't want to be a farmer in rural

Canada, either. Dad had a knack for sales. He didn't know where that would take him in life.

Dad was as ambitious as a dog digging for a buried bone. He thought, "I must make more money, gain fame, and power." He was itching to get out of Winnipeg, nicknamed "Winterpeg." The city has exceedingly long, bitter winters. I don't know whether he was still a hardware store helper. But what I know is he needed to go to a big city to make more money.

In the early 1920s, my father bolted from the family. He was the first child that left. A young man of twenty, Dad said goodbye Winnipeg, also called "Chicago of the North," and hello to the real Chicago. Dad may have heard that there were jobs available from brother Louis, a Chicago tailor. Dad moved without a job and was resolved to find one.

But he discovered that jobs were scarce in Chicago. This is not what Dad expected. Chicago, as well as the nation, was in a deep, short-lived economic depression. U.S. unemployment peaked at 12 percent. Many returning World War I veterans still had not found employment.

Everything happened quickly and grandly in Chicago since the 1910s. The city grew with incredible speed. Its population exploded. Blacks fled the Jim Crow South in the thousands in search of industrial jobs. They brought jazz and hopes of the American Dream into my black neighborhood. Russian Jews quickly migrated to

Chicago, too, making up 80 percent of Chicago's Jewish population by 1930.

Yet, Dad landed a job seemingly overnight. He started selling plumbing equipment on the road for the suspicious Miller Supply Company. Joe's boss was once indicted by a federal grand jury on a fraud charge. I was surprised Dad found a job so fast under those circumstances.

An unverified family story says that lifelong friend Tony Palermo helped Joe get the job. It's not clear if that was Dominick "Tootsie" Palermo, head of the crime syndicate for Chicago's south suburbs, bordering Indiana. Joe worked in Indiana when he married Mom. They then lived on the South Side of Chicago. Palermo was convicted for extorting protection money in Indiana in 1991. Something smells fishy here—Joe and Tootsie Palermo were both connected to south Chicago and Indiana. Hmmm.

Mom, on the other hand, had a squeaky-clean past. Bessie was born in 1905 in Glasgow, Scotland, one of seven children of Russian-born parents, Louis Shear and Rachel Gutnick. I called Rachel my little grandma and Dad's mother, Bessie Sheps, my big grandma. She was much bigger than Rachel. Even with Russian heritage, Mom and Dad spoke flawless English, never Yiddish or a foreign language, and didn't have accents. Mom's father was a tailor.

At age five, Mom and her birth family immigrated from Scotland to Calgary, Canada, some 500 miles north of Montana. Nicknamed Cowtown for its famous Calgary Stampede, Calgary is now modern and known for farming, high altitude baking, and the oil industry. After a dozen years in Calgary, the Shears moved to Chicago.

Mom and Dad both separately moved from Canada to Chicago. I don't know how they met. But I do know they fell head over heels for each other right away. Love is so influential it can make you do crazy things. Joe and Bessie yearned for marriage at once. They eloped. They married in 1923 in Crown Point, Indiana, a Chicago border town known for quickie weddings by justices of the peace. Joe, twenty-one, of nearby Hammond, was a clerk. Bessie, seventeen and a half, of Chicago, was a typist.

Joe was of legal age to marry, but Bessie was underage. She had to be eighteen. She could be younger with parental consent, but I doubt she got that. City clerks did not always follow the laws. Dad probably sweet-talked the clerk—likely a female—and told her he was a clerk too. Why rush and get married? Just overwhelmed by love? It wasn't pregnancy out of wedlock. Their first child, Morley, wasn't conceived until four months after the marriage. Morley was born in 1924, and I was born three years after him.

Before age thirteen, I discovered that I shared some traits with Dad, such as perfectionism and determination. I was a young, impressionable child. I watched my parents or older brother as they did something and imitated their behavior. I did what I wanted, though.

I didn't want to be like Dad or follow in his footsteps in business. We had different interests. Dad had a high school education and did not pursue finer things in life as I did. I set my sights on being autonomous and had a desire to help people grow.

In the early 1940s, I started spending more time away from home with friends. I had a psychological understanding of my role in my original family. Dr. Gradle operated on my eyes many times. They were over, and I felt invigorated physically. I was in a new and different life with my pals. I became more mature, insightful, and at peace with myself and the environment.

From the very beginning, my life ran in circles. I was always needing something, then getting into new situations trying to find it, and hoping to return to my comfort zone, having been transformed. Thank goodness, I had Mom. She gave me confidence. She always reminded me, "Have faith . . . things will be better tomorrow."

I needed a lot of Mom's assurance for what would happen next after birth in a new, out of the ordinary world.

CHAPTER 3:
Overcoming My Demons

I lit up the room when I was born. It seemed like I waved a magic wand. My parents were more hopeful, happier, and purposeful than before. I gave them a big reason they should lead productive and well-ordered lives.

Dad became a dignified American citizen a few years after my birth. He Americanized his name, changing it from Jacob to Joseph, or as he laughed, "Just call me Joe." My father aimed to own a home and business and to give his children opportunities to succeed in life.

It seemed like I, as a baby, made everything better in my family. But no. I made it worse. I was a baby with serious eye problems, a crisis that no one could immediately solve. Chuck Palahniuk, in his novel, *Lullaby*, wrote, "I've learned that, in every story, there is a big, bad something. An evil force that, no matter the size, corrupts the world of the story, and tries its best to destroy the hero. A wolf, a witch, a giant, a dragon, a knight . . . or an idea, a desire, a temptation . . . or even a book."

I felt like the hero, Jack in *Jack and the Beanstalk*, setting out to destroy "a great evil threatening the land" (the Giant). Only the Giant was inside of me, my blindness gnawing at my mind and body. My big question: Could I survive this life-changing conflict and find happiness every day? I needed better eyesight, and I tried to get it.

My journey from immaturity to self-realization took me to some dark, weird places. I fought to solve the predicament. My misfortune was escalating, and the stakes were soaring. I went in and out of two worlds—medicine/surgery and fantasy. First, I entered an intimidating, mysterious new world full of frightening uncertainties, unusual language, and high hopes. It was a peculiar world of ophthalmologists, optometrists, and opticians.

My parents found the best Chicago doctor for me. He was Dr. Harry S. Gradle, forty-four, who was on the staff at the hospital where I was born. Dr. Gradle was an internationally known eye surgeon and leader in the prevention of blindness.

New babies usually do not have sharp vision, but they can see their mother's image. I didn't have any vision because of cataracts.

Dr. Gradle removed cataracts from both my eyes before I was only two months old, a crucial stage of vision development. My parents hoped the surgery would save my sight. But it was a marathon over the next several years, rehabilitating my eyes and mind. I wore expensive, thick Coke-bottle-type eyeglasses and other special glasses. Contact lenses were not yet available for the public. Cataract surgery today gives some kids 20/20 vision and driving vision. All I got was Coke-bottle glasses and the hope of walking-around vision.

Before age three, I purposely broke dozens of eyeglasses. They were awfully uncomfortable. Every pair that Mom gave me, I took them off my head and threw them hard on the wood floor. SHCHING! The glass shattered, went into every nook and cranny of the room, and was heard throughout the residence. "Not again," Mom exclaimed, "What did you do that for? These are to help you." Shaking a fist, Dad roared louder, "Don't do that again. These glasses cost a lot of money." I cried my eyes dry. Finally, I realized glasses helped me see, and I didn't break them anymore.

By four or five, my eyes had developed enough for an eye chart test. I'll never forget the results. Mom hoped I wouldn't be diagnosed as blind. The doctor reported that I was legally blind. I wasn't completely blind. Still, Mom's breathing stopped for a split second.

I was actually born with two rare eye conditions for babies—cataracts and posterior synechiae. Posterior synechiae is a scar-like tissue that closes the pupil. The cause of the condition is unknown.

PART 1 SOMETHING'S VERY WRONG

My pupils just didn't develop properly—one is much smaller than the other. Pupils are so important. They start the sight process. They control the amount of light that gets into the eye. Dr. Gradle invented needling surgery, which enlarged my pupils or kept them open. The doctor stuck sharp needles into my eyes while I was under anesthesia. Just thinking of having a needle go into my eye made me shiver. But it was painless. The aftercare was the problem. After each operation, I stayed in the hospital for three days. The doctor operated on only one eye each time I went to the hospital.

After surgery, I wore an eye bandage and eye patch until I went home. My eye was very sticky and itchy. Mom squawked as I rubbed them. She advised me, "Lay still, and don't move your head." Mom, I argued, "I can't do that. It's too hard." I was a highly active child. I asked Mom: "When am I getting out of here? I can't stand it. I want to go home and play with Esther on the swings!" I felt the surgeries would never stop.

Eye surgeries ruined my summer vacations. After cataract surgery, I was hospitalized thirteen times before my tenth birthday for needling. Dr. Gradle needled my left eye seven times and my right eye six times. That's more than one hospital stay each summer or a total of forty days over that awful decade. If I wasn't in the hospital, I might be roaming downtown Chicago, with little parental supervision or even concern.

CHAPTER 3 Overcoming My Demons

By age ten, I looked forward to going to the hospital with Mom. That was a wonderful time. I'd have Mom to myself. She'd read to me from my favorite book, *Alice in Wonderland,* and from *The Wizard of Oz.* She didn't do this at home. She was so busy with two other young kids, cooking, baking, cleaning, and managing the house.

That time alone with Mom gave me a respite when I privately reflected on the instability of our family. Our family moved seven times in my first ten years. Dad searched for work during the Great Depression, one of the darkest economic times in American history. Dad lost his job as a Chicago traveling plumbing supplies salesman. He and half the families were scraping to survive.

Dad had just seventy-five dollars left in his pocket. He told Mom, "We can't get by here on our own. We're moving to Drumheller and living with your brothers." Dad didn't know it, but the worldwide Depression hit Canada even harder! I don't think Dad found a job in Drumheller.

No matter where I lived, people frequently stared at me squinting and looking blind. They'd ask, "Are you really blind?" I'd say, "I'm proud to be legally blind. Judge me by my abilities and accomplishments, not by my disability."

I wouldn't let this discrimination make me feel like a second-class citizen. Actually, my disability or visual impairment empowered me. I don't see as well as most people. But I can do everything a seeing person can on my own—communicate on electronic devices, dress, eat, and experience the same feelings. Most importantly, I've led a better life than many people. My life's been fulfilling, loving, and delightful. Amazing to lots of folks.

Eyesight in America is a big problem. Some 27 million adults report trouble seeing, even with glasses or contact lenses, or can't see at all, according to a 2017 federal survey. I'm among about one million Americans who are legally blind. I'm living in a gray world—between fully sighted and totally blind people. Born with legal blindness, I never had normal eyesight. I read my iPhone or a piece of paper a couple inches from my eyes. Anything further away—lights, shapes, colors, large objects, and people—will be out of focus.

How's my vision compared to yours? If you have normal 20/20 vision, you can stand twenty feet from a standard eye chart and read the top eight lines of letters. I can only see the top letter "E" with less than 20/200 vision in both eyes with glasses and contact lenses. I'm not allowed to drive a vehicle in most places. I've never driven. I can take my wheeled walker anywhere without a guide dog or long white cane. Before marriage, I went anywhere by myself. Now, a friend or relative guides me.

Limited vision—and now age—never stopped me from living a full life. I had my father's resolve to succeed at anything, even if it was hard. My friends never excluded me from any activities. I played baseball with the boys. I couldn't see a ball hit to me until it almost reached me. One time I tried to catch a fly ball with a mitt, but it hit my finger, which was swollen for a week.

The most important thing that happened to me as a youngster was my sixth birthday party. That was the first birthday I really remember. Mom threw the party. She asked me, "Faith, what food do you want to have at the party?" I told her, "Chocolate cake, red jello, and ice cream."

We lived then in Drumheller, above Aunt Nettie's and Uncle Rube's general store. That was much better than our earlier place, a small, kerosene-stinking cabin. Jewish families in the area usually owned general stores. Mom conveniently went downstairs and got food from her uncle. I worshiped sweets—ate ice cream and candy all the time. But never got fat. I was so active I just burned up the calories.

My Uncle Jack and Aunt Gertie ran the town's candy store. Of course, it was my favorite place to go. I always overindulged on candy dots that you pulled off paper strips. When parents lost their kids, they always found them at the candy store.

After Mom took my party food order, she asked, "What gifts do you want?" I replied, "I really want a blue bike so badly and a Chinese flowered parasol." It turned out to be an ideal party. I got everything I asked for. During the party, I let out happy bursts of screaming, shouting, laughter, squeals, and giggles. I kept begging Mom, "Can I please go ride my bike now?" It was really a tricycle, my first bike. Before the party was over, I rode it up and down the street, holding the open parasol over my head. I peddled as fast as I could, waving the paper parasol. The wind snapped the parasol into two pieces. Waaaaah! Waaaaah! Waaaaah! Mom came running up to me. We hugged. But she couldn't stop my crying.

This birthday was so important to me. For the first time in my life, I felt special. I got a warm feeling that I was really an exceptional person in the family. My parents granted all my wishes. I fancied being the current center of attention instead of Morley. Mom and Dad had devoted a lot of time to him. My younger sister Shelly (Rochelle) was born a month after the party. Then she got all of my parents' attention.

I cherished happy times like these with the family. But I didn't know how long they'd last. Were they doing all this for me since my future was questionable? I mean with my vision handicap. Afterward, I rode my bike all around town. By myself, with no one watching me. No adults. Those were the days kids could play everywhere, with no supervision, until the sun went down. Sometimes even later.

I adored Drumheller. I was happy and carefree. I was surrounded by friendly people and warmed by special event bonfires. I biked to the bonfires. I hated to leave town. The next year, we moved to Calgary, where Mom's sister, my Aunt Belle, lived.

After one year of living in Calgary, I woke up one Monday early before school and couldn't find my bike. I ran to Mom: "Where's my bike?" Mom: "Faith, we had to sell it." Dad gave me my first bike, then took it away a year later. He sold it with their belongings for cash to move back to Chicago. My parents promised me they wouldn't sell my bike. But they did anyway. How could I believe them anymore? I thought they no longer appreciated me. I asked, "How could you do that?" They lamented, "We're sorry. It's gone, and we can't get it back."

The shock hit me then. I was crushed with sorrow. I fell down on the floor, curled up in a ball, and sobbed until I was exhausted and could hardly get my breath. The little blue tricycle that fit me like a glove was gone forever. I can still see me riding it down the street carrying the parasol. I never forgave Mom and Dad for selling my bike.

They also sold my small little alphabet table too. I had fond memories of playing with Polly and my other dolls at the table. It had all the alphabet letters on its porcelain top. I sat at the table and sang the alphabet song, "A-B-C-D-E-F-G . . . " I was sure they'd sell that dumb table. But not my bike! Our family—still penniless—drove back to Chicago and lived with my grandparents, Mom's parents.

After a two-year absence, I saw Dr. Gradle. I worried I'd have to have more surgery. But I liked going to the doctor's office. It was more time alone with Mom. And she made it fun. I always waited at least three hours before I saw the doctor. I felt I waited forever. Dr. Gradle was famous, swamped, and overbooked.

He was one of those old-fashioned doctors who cared more about his patients than his profit. Dr. Gradle never rushed through talking with Mom and me. He didn't worry about his time schedule. Mother packed books, toys, and lunch for me to keep me busy in the waiting room. I tightly held my favorite doll, Polly, or sometimes I put her down and played with the doctor's marbles or a beads game.

On every visit, Mom made me use my eyes while waiting. Either I'd read or look at picture books. I couldn't sit still. I was the type of kid who liked to run, do, jump, and play.

When I got bored, Mom would say, "Come over here to the window and stand on this chair." The doctor's office was on the eighth floor in the historic Reliance Building in the Loop in downtown Chicago. It overlooked busy Michigan Avenue, Lake Shore Drive, and Lake Michigan in the distance.

Starting the conversation with Mom, I said,

— *It's pretty out there.*

— What do you see, Faith?

— *I see cars, I see boats, and I see a blue lake.*

— Look at the sky too. What do the clouds look like?

CHAPTER 3 Overcoming My Demons

Mom helped me recognize cloud shapes. My imagination was always at work.

— *Look, Mom, I see a bear.*

— Where is it?

— *Over there*, pointing with my finger.

Later, I used what I learned from Mom. I'd said to my girlfriend, "Oh, look at the elephant over there in the clouds." The shocked friend: "What the hell are you talking about!"

Mom asked me to look from the sky out to the lake.

— What do you see on the lake? Tell me how many sailboats you can see.

— *There's one sailboat, there's two . . .*

The lake was pretty far away, but I could see the boats better than the cars. If I missed a boat, Mom said, "Did you see that one over on the left?" If I got restless counting boats, she'd ask questions about the cars.

From eight floors up, I could see the small cars but not their colors.

— Tell me how many cars do you see right now going down the street?

— Do you see a red car down there?

— Let's count how many red cars go by in the next couple of minutes.

— *Mom, I can't do it!*

— Yes, you can. There are red ones down there.

Mom had new techniques and made the time go quicker. I think Mom's what-do-you-see game helped me see different shades of green in leaves today. That was pretty damn gutsy in front of other patients. I was afraid waiting-room patients would comment on our game. But I never heard them. Mother stopped the counting games by age six or seven. Instead, we'd look at magazine pictures together, or I'd play with office toys.

I don't know how Dad paid for my hefty medical expenses for a decade during the Depression. Relatives must have helped. Many people couldn't support their families, much less pay medical and hospital costs.

In 1937, I received terrible and good news, and Mom made a decision that opened my eyes to the world around me. After the last needling procedure, Dr. Gradle gave Mom and me the sad news: "We can't make the pupils any bigger." I could see but not clearly. This meant I'd be legally blind for the rest of my life and might be a heavy burden on my family and community. The good news: The needling surgeries were over, and, at age ten, I could get on with my life and celebrate with a big dish of ice cream.

I didn't find the cure that I sought. And the numerous surgeries caused anxiety and physical stress. Now I wondered as I returned to a non-surgical life if the medical world had changed me personally.

CHAPTER 3 Overcoming My Demons

I was doing poorly in school. I couldn't see as well as the other kids. I went to six elementary schools in four years in Chicago and Canada. I finally learned to read by age six. Some kids had started reading before me. When we moved back to Chicago, Mom sent me to a special public school for children with vision problems. I discovered a fresh outlook on life and a new peculiar friend like me at Leander Stone School. The school was different than my other schools. My homeroom special ed teacher helped me complete classwork that I couldn't normally do with my disability.

In third grade, I met an offbeat girl, Esther. We became inseparable. Kids called us Mutt and Jeff, like the characters in the comic strip, *Mutt and Jeff*. I was tall and thin, and she was short and chunky. We were much alike and became lifelong close friends. We both enjoyed things more suited to boys. Our hair was messy. But we were smart and had insatiable curiosities about our world.

We brought our lunch to school. Esther would bring vegetables. I brought a sandwich, fruit, and cookies. One day I asked, "What are you eating?' "Cabbage," she answered. Me: "You've got to be kidding! Who eats raw cabbage? That's rabbit food!" Esther countered, "I love it. Want to have some?" I said, "No, thanks." She said, "Try it. You might like it." I didn't like it at first. But by the end of the year, I ate the raw cabbage that she shared with me.

Today, we no longer share those memories. She died in 2013. I deeply miss her.

Finally, I discovered a life-changing secret that was right under my nose all along. It was Mom's positivity and Dad's grit. They taught me never to quit and that things will always be better tomorrow! That attitude helped me beat the monster inside of me. But I experienced a trail of acute emotional suffering.

After my surgeries, I was a new person. I went through physical and psychological repair and healed emotionally. I now had more self-confidence and felt stronger that nothing ever will slow me down in life, even disability.

But would my positivity work in the next different place that I entered—the mystical world?

CHAPTER 4:
Faith in Wonderland

When I was five, I fell into a fantasy world. I was trying to manage two unfamiliar situations at once—the worlds of medicine and fantasy. I didn't know whether my eyesight would get any better. But I hoped the mystical promised land would be a place where I could live happily ever after.

I was obsessed with *Alice in Wonderland*, the 1865 fairytale book by Lewis Carroll. It's a dream about a little girl who follows the White Rabbit down a rabbit hole. She finds a place filled with outlandish creatures and bizarre incidents and wakes up after a pack of cards attacks her. A rabbit hole is a metaphor for an entry into an increasingly peculiar dilemma. The book is the story of Alice growing up, realizing the power of her imagination. For me, it was trying to survive childhood with severely impaired vision.

PART 1 SOMETHING'S VERY WRONG

Mom must have read the book to me 101 times while I was in the hospital for eye surgery and at home. I'd say, "Mommy, reread that part about the Queen of Hearts when she said, 'Off with their heads!'" I could recite lines from the book before I could read. I've read the book as an adult too. It's my favorite book ever.

I was fascinated with Carroll's Jabberwocky nonsensical poem in *Through the Looking-Glass*, the sequel to *Wonderland*. It was about the killing of an eponymous monster called the Jabberwock.

As an adult, I reread the Jabberwocky poem and discovered its hidden meaning. It was about me and my life! It was about me overcoming the demon (my vision loss), as the young boy in the poem. The hero (me, the heroine) leaves home and goes out into the world (sees an eye specialist) and faces an evil force (legal blindness). She tackles several challenges (many eye operations) that test her bravery. But she finally defeats the monster that looks like a dragon. And she then comes home again as the heroine.

Alice and I were so much alike. We were both individualistic, curious, imaginative, strong-willed, honest, and adventurous. We both liked orange marmalade. While falling down the rabbit hole, Alice grabbed an empty jar of marmalade, my favorite. Both of us dared to question what the characters expected of us. Alice inspired me to follow my own natural curiosities and adventuresome nature, no matter what may happen.

CHAPTER 4 Faith in Wonderland

One day I dreamed of being Faith in my own book, "Faith in Wonderland." Like Alice, I fell asleep, saw the White Rabbit scurry down a rabbit hole, and followed him.

I searched for a way out of my rabbit hole. But I got lost in a unique world. I was an incredibly young girl and didn't know how to get home. I met new, creepy characters and endured impossible situations. My external and internal scuffles grew more intimate, personal, and devastating. I couldn't get out of Wonderland, and that upset me.

But I got back to the way things were earlier before my world was tipped upside down. I barely survived, adjusted to sudden change, and got home. I was too young to defend myself. I had to get home quickly. But the world locked all the doors. I did something, and the world did something back.

I might die from starvation or exposure. The Queen of Hearts was going to execute me too. I realized I could end my dream by waking up. I woke from my dream and was dropped back into real life. But I woke with a pack of cards sitting on the stand next to my bed. Was it really a dream?

Both Alice's and my journeys are really about our difficulties growing up. Unprejudiced and innocent, we're on quests to find our identity. We try hard to endure the confusing adult world. The people had silly regulations, unquestioned social etiquette, big egos, and bad habits.

PART 1 SOMETHING'S VERY WRONG

You can't live long in a dream world like this without losing sanity, identity, laws, and logic. I longed for the world of common sense and consciousness—home. Yet, the images from my surreal, nonsensical fantasy dream crept into my memory. And if it's in my mind, it seemed real to me. I lived in my dream memory for several years. Like Alice, I got out of the hole with confusing doubts about my mixed-up, crazy world.

After my adventure, I just meant to return home like an average person. But I wasn't. I stood out, paradoxically, by fitting in. I just aimed to be healthy—my normalcy quest. Yet, I was quirky. I wore eclectic clothing, frilly white dresses on the playground, and did daring things with the boys.

I liked to do what the boys did—play baseball, roughhouse on the playground, climb trees and games like daredevil, king of the hill, red rover, and tag. Boys' contests were the best. I was socially awkward with my vision loss. I merely needed to be with people who didn't care about it. Some people thought I was immature and even troubled.

Mom dressed me very girly for first and second grades. She insisted on me wearing shiny polished shoes and impeccably-ironed frilly, layered pink and white dresses. I was one of the prettiest-dressed school girls. After school, I looked like a ragamuffin. I was black from head to toe— my dress, socks and shoes, my hands and my scraped knees. I'd play as hard as the boys and didn't care if I got dirty.

My dresses got the dirtiest of all the kids. I fell the most playing tag and red rover. I tripped over my barely visible feet and uneven ground. I'd play on the cinder playground during recess. The cinders were charred coal ashes, a brownish, but not black color. I'd also play in the dirt. Mom shouted at me, "You did it again, you're filthy." I replied, "I'm sorry, Mommy. But the playground is dirty." The next day, though, Mom sent me back to school in another crisp, clean dress.

I didn't hate all girly things, though. I had feminine interests too. I liked the color pink and was delighted to play with my dolls. I was always playing with something as a kid—regular dolls, paper dolls, and the boys. I got all the toys I ever imagined. I played with dolls if I was going to be home alone, and if I were out, I'd rather play with boys.

By age eight, something unreal happened. I started getting absorbed in building architecture. I was attracted to my doctor's historic office building lobby and my neighborhood movie theaters. I've always been interested in my surroundings. Again, I think it's my mom's influence.

I looked forward to Saturdays. We'd go to the movies and eat candy and ice cream. It was the early Golden Age period of Hollywood, with Judy Garland, Clark Gable, and Shirley Temple.

PART 1 SOMETHING'S VERY WRONG

One day in the mid-1930s, something memorable happened at my nearest movie theaters. I walked from home in a busy shopping district to two movie theaters in the West Garfield Park neighborhood on the West Side of Chicago. What caught my eye at the Paradise Theater was not the movies, like Shirley Temple's *The Littlest Rebel*. It was the ornate architecture at the Paradise, billed as the world's most beautiful theater. I saw large objects, people, and color at a distance, but they were out of focus.

As a third-grader, I was fascinated by its sheer opulence, intricate craftsmanship, and its endless 3,600 seats. I squinted my eyes, looking up at its blue ceiling with shiny stars. The nearby Marbro Theater, with almost 4,000 seats, furthered my appreciation of building architecture. It was made in the Spanish Baroque style, including a flashy terra-cotta facade. I was awed by its massive stage, proscenium arch, and two-story lobby. It had a marble staircase and small tree-sized European crystal chandelier. Boy, would I have dug sliding down the banister there!

I was curious and impressionable. I explored all public areas of these theaters. Imagine me telling my mother, "Mom, I'm going to the movies to see the theater's architecture!" Looking back, studying these two theaters was the start of a new phase in my life.

Overnight, my days took a surprising twist. I came to a fork-in-the-road moment.

CHAPTER 4 Faith in Wonderland

In my awareness phase of childhood, I discovered what would alter my life. I arrived at a decision in several ways. I pieced together clues from my movie and Stone School experiences. My wits—the mental resources of intelligent observation, keen perception, and ingenious contrivance (my creative wrinkle). My grit—my tenacity to overcome my growing eyesight crisis and pursuit of my creative talents. Stone School grew my interest in the arts—theater, music, literature, painting, and sculpture. These are activities attracting people with skill and imagination. They were like me, creative and imaginative.

During my five years at Stone, classmates and I went on many weekly special enrichment school trips to plays, operas, concerts, and museums. At school, we watched educational films, performers, and guest speakers one morning a week. We went to every museum in Chicago. I saw my first opera, *Aida*, wearing a long dress on the opening night of the Metropolitan Opera. I was fascinated by the stories of live productions. I was amazed the actors learned all those lines. I never expected this to happen to nine-year-old me.

Esther also nurtured my fondness for culture. Esther and I often spent whole weekend days together at the new, fascinating Museum of Science and Industry on the South Side. We took two buses to get there. The museum's first exhibit was an actual coal mine. A few years earlier, I lived in Drumheller, a coal-mining town. We were both pretty smart, and we found it irresistible challenging each other to answer questions asked by the hands-on exhibits. Like, "How does coal power our lights?"

I made a discovery from a decision I made. It was unforeseen. I came to the proverbial fork in the road. There was something symbolic about this that got my imagination going. I had to make a life-changing decision. One route I called "Tomboy," and the other way was "Highbrow." I'm a big baseball fan, and I remember what a famous player-coach-manager, Yogi Berra, proclaimed: "When you come to a fork in the road, take it." He meant that life is full of choices and that we need to make them. We need to keep moving forward.

One day, I announced to Mom, "I'm turning over a new leaf. No more tomboy stuff for me. I love the arts." I became an art and cultural aficionado in fourth grade! That surprised my family. They saw me enjoying childhood and having fun playing with the boys. If I didn't make that decision, I might have grown up being labeled a tomboy, who many people think are lesbians, even though it's not true. But then the world never looked so good to me.

I never regretted my decision. I've soaked up arts and educational travel like a sponge. The world opened up, and I explored much of it. It's helped me through difficulties in life. Going to Stone School was one of the best things that ever happened to me.

CHAPTER 4 Faith in Wonderland

It was worth it, even though I had to take two electric-powered streetcars to get to school and another two to get home by myself. Some cold, snowy days, I felt the streetcar would never come. When it did, I faced a crowded, uncomfortable, jostling ride. Riding a tram, I thought of myself as an adult teenager. While other girls were coping with cliques and pajama parties, I was absorbing culture, making new friends, and fighting rush hour traffic.

I found my way out of the surgery and fantasy worlds and took control of my destiny. I accidentally discovered that I had a passion for cultural arts. I grew personally using many potent lessons I found in a mysterious hole in the ground. I was growing up and realizing the power of imagination and curiosity. The experiences shaped my life with internal discovery (my brother treats me as his best friend) and external resolution (eye operations and fantasy trips were over).

My wild journey to an unusual place helped me survive childhood and saved my life! I enjoyed the fun of childhood without being relegated to the blind world. But the world wore me down from feeling so many emotions—confusion, anger, love, sadness, joy, fear, and surprise.

Stone School molded my life. I finally learned how to achieve with my legally blind eyes and enjoy living. Things couldn't be more ideal. I couldn't wait to hit the streets and begin my new existence.

PART 1 SOMETHING'S VERY WRONG

In Faith in Wonderland, I grew personally. I learned philosophy and morals that enriched my life. Mom's the-sun-will-come-out-tomorrow outlook prevented me from going insane after all my eye operations. Mom would say to me quite often, "Faith, no matter what happens in your life, you need to find joy every day. Look how lucky you are. I'm here for you. I'll always be here for you, and I'll be here to read to you. You're going to be okay.

"Tomorrow is another day. Every day is a new beginning. You're going to wake up and enjoy the day. It's going to be a bright day. And you're going to use all of it productively."

Mom and I were eternal optimists. I was forever changed and always capable of creating change. Mom taught me never to give up, no matter what. They say positivity affects mental and physical health. That's why I'm so healthy at ninety-two years of age. You, too, can change your life for the better, no matter how difficult it is. Turn negative into positive experiences. Every day is a new beginning. Enjoy it!

After Wonderland, I returned home at the end of the Great Depression and created a new me. I became more resilient through adversity. They say, "What doesn't kill you makes you stronger." I overcame legal blindness and suffering in a flawed family. My eye problems turned a little girl into feeling like a young adult. I was advanced for my age. I started a new journey in the real world in familiar surroundings. Mom still supported me and was now raising Shelly, four, Daddy's new girl. Dad was off working all hours of the day at his new plumbing business. Morley, thirteen, and I were best pals.

Still, I didn't have a pleasant homecoming.

My family had moved again. This time we moved to a small, one-bedroom third-floor apartment without air conditioning in a Jewish neighborhood on the North Side of Chicago. It was in the Uptown Community neighborhood, once a wealthy area that deteriorated considerably during the Depression.

Shelly and I shared the bedroom, Mom and Dad slept on a Murphy in-a-door bed in the living room, and Morley had a couch in the dining room. I went to a little porch off the kitchen to get privacy, where I thought about where I've been, and if I could survive in the ordinary world.

I was thrilled that we could walk to Lake Michigan's Foster Avenue Beach on Lake Shore Drive, now a famous beach in the Edgewater section. On sweltering summer nights, we kids even slept overnight in the park there. We didn't even think that we could be robbed, molested, or murdered. Crime rates were declining. Capone was in prison for tax evasion. And the economy was recovering from the Depression and Prohibition. I was thrilled that family and friends surrounded me.

I was a completely changed person. I was amazed at my transformation. I underwent a physical renewal—my eyes were healing from surgical operations. My mind was more precise. I psychologically understood I would be legally blind forever. I emotionally healed and was rid of my *Wonderland* fears of growing up and the danger of curiosity. I suffered so much. I felt a spiritual awakening was controlling me and watching over me.

I found that cultural arts helped me make sense of the world and helped change me in many ways. I:

- Discovered more than one solution to life's problems. In school, it was correct answers. In art, it was sound judgments.
- Learned how to empathize with people, especially as I wrote poetry and became a better person.
- Showed my individuality in cooking.
- Found confidence and learned from mistakes in high school theater and on the debating team.
- Determined that perseverance was the only way I could play the violin by creating larger notes that I could see on the sheet music.
- Wrote poetry or stories and saw paintings in galleries and museums that enabled me to express emotions.
- Danced to music that lifted me up.
- Kept my mind alert.
- Got lost in a work's beauty, allowing me to put aside problems.
- Stimulated my curiosity about paintings' subjects.

- Became more creative and think on my feet.

I found my mission in life: loving arts and culture, communicating, and making the world a better place.

When I was almost a teenager, one of the greatest lessons Mom taught me is that everyone makes mistakes. I sometimes burnt cookies baking with Mom. That was okay. She taught me to try again and do it differently, so the cookies turned out yummy.

A big question often ran through my mind: Could I take the new me into the real world and survive with my family and friends? Who wants to deal with a visually impaired, flawed person like me? Could I find joy every day with what I learned?

My attitude helped me achieve a near-impossible thing—appearing healthy with only one-tenth of standard eyesight.

I thought, "Be yourself. Don't worry about what others think of you." People say about me, "She's a little weird." I wanted to be like other kids. But I wasn't. To this day, I'm a little eccentric and very private. I don't want anyone taking care of me. That's just being myself.

By the end of the depressing 1930s, I really needed someone to hug. So did our country. I hugged my wooden Shirley Temple doll, and the nation embraced her in the movies. The actress was my age and my favorite movie performer. Somehow the doll's feet rotted. Mom told me to throw my Shirley Temple doll out, and I did. I was depressed for a few days. Yet, I bounced back. I was a cheerful child with a sunny outlook on life. People just wanted to hug me. I had an insatiable curiosity and knew more about the world than you'd expect.

I was only a twelve-year-old kid hoping that something good would happen soon.

Everything was quiet at home. I felt it was too peaceful, like the calm before the storm. Then, surprise! Suddenly, a big rainstorm hit us.

Little did I know how bad it would be.

PART 2:
WAS DAD A BAD SEED?
(1940-1965)

[Page Intentionally Blank]

CHAPTER 5:
My Family, Myself

After my birth, our family celebrated a wave of national patriotism. Singer Kate Smith sang an old Irving Berlin song never performed in public before—*God Bless America*. As the Depression effects lingered, world disaster struck. With particular meaning to us as Jews, Germany invaded Poland in 1939, starting World War II.

At the same time, our family faced an outbreak of chaos. I was a six-year-old off-center child, being shaped and scarred by my abnormal family. We really couldn't always get along with each other very well—especially with Dad. He set inflexible conventions that created tension and a lack of reliance and love in the family.

I ultimately became an emotionally vulnerable adult, obsessed with perfection. Dad and I had a love-hate relationship. I always was afraid of not living up to his extremely high standards. Dad's mentality made it hard for him to slow down or be fun-loving and romantic with Mom.

We were one big, screwed-up family.

Family allegiances kept us at a distance. Mom and I were close. Dad favored Morley (heir to his business) and Shelly. I was tight with Morley, my real father figure. Mom, the apron matron, held the family together. Wage earner Dad, the patriarch, oozed authority wherever he went and was aloof with me.

Only eight, I had a family disaster on my hands. First, the world denied me healthy eyesight, and now it deprived me of a traditional family. I saw close, loving, and supportive families in my neighborhood and in my school chums' homes. I wanted a family that celebrated successes of family members that had more positive interactions than negative ones, and that loved each other and stayed close. Ideal families were dangled right in front of me. I wanted one too.

My venture intensified as I searched for ways to solve my strife at home. It was an uphill battle that I might fail. I was an adorably precocious child who found a confidant in Morley. He taught me how to support myself without help, have fun, and forget that Daddy was never around. Morley saw me defy authority, get disciplined, and keep coming back for more. He should see me now, strictly obeying all rules and laws.

CHAPTER 5 My Family, Myself

When adults weren't around, I couldn't help being mischievous and sneaky. One time my parents went on vacation, and I boldly helped paint every room of the house in a different bright color. The kitchen was bright yellow; the dining room, chartreuse; Shelly's and my bedroom, shocking pink; Mom and Dad's bedroom, soft blue; and the living room, bright blue. Mom only remarked, "Oh, it's so bright." I was surprised Dad didn't discipline all of us. But we all had to live with it for many years.

If I weren't getting into tight spots, I'd be eating confections. At age nine, I found someone who paid for my ice cream habit in Chicago on the West Side. It was Uncle Sam, whose family lived with us in Chicago. Four or five times a week, he gave Morley and me each fifteen cents for large, three-scoop ice cream cones from the corner drugstore on Grenshaw Street.

I'd pick my three favorite flavors—chocolate, strawberry, and my very favorite, peppermint, on the bottom. I'd finally get to the peppermint, but I usually was so full I couldn't finish the cone.

Mom dearly loved her kids and only loved one man, Dad, in her entire life. Bulky and short, she was kind, clean, a great cook, and was always smiling with a positive outlook on life. Mom was my biggest supporter: "I'm so proud of you; you're doing good . . . Don't let anything get in the way of what you want. I'm here for you whenever you need me. I'll be your cheerleader no matter what." She inspired my siblings and me always to find joy.

I called her a miracle homemaker. Full of energy, she was raising three kids plus spending seven or eight hours a day on housework, finances, repairs, and errands. She had little help. Dad never helped around the house. She never asked us kids to help, except wash dinner dishes. The first time I washed clothes was after I was married. Our maid Bertha helped Mom cook and clean for several years.

I never sewed or crocheted. I told Mom, I couldn't thread a needle. My vision was not good enough for that. Mom made many of my clothes from childhood into my sixties: lovely knitted dresses, knitted coats, and sweaters. If I were going on a date, I'd say to Mom, "Gee, Mom, I don't know what I'm going to wear." She giggled, "Well, Faith, I'll make a nice little dress for you." When she wasn't cleaning or sewing, Mom often played poker and the rummy card game Kalooki with Aunt Belle for money, sometimes twice a day. Regularly she'd serve us kids dinner, then go out and play cards. We put ourselves to bed.

Mom's body finally gave out at age eighty-eight. She never complained of her failing kidneys and heart and painful bones riddled with cancer.

Complete opposites, Mom and Dad remade my life in ways I never realized until now. Mom made me what I am today—like her, positive, resourceful, and brave. Dad, stringent and cold, taught me to be tenacious.

People professed, "You can't go to Europe alone." I did with Donna, both age twenty. Everybody thought we were crazy. It was uncommon then for two young ladies to do that. Mom, when I announced our plans: "I think it's wonderful. If you don't have enough money, I'll help you." Dad commented, "That's foolish. You're too young to go."

He was an absentee dad who worked long and hard developing his home-building business. He was up at five, out of the house by six, and not home until after dinner. We kids needed a poppa at home. We expected Dad to come home for dinner, but he missed dinner much of the time. "We can't wait any longer for Dad," said Mom, probably knowing he wouldn't be there. "We'll have to go ahead and eat without him."

My mother was the good mom, the parent who got things right. She would yell at me sometimes ("Wash your hands before dinner!"), but she rarely criticized me. Instead, Mom often suggested better ways to do things. I did this with my adopted daughter, Naomi, too. Once Naomi wanted to quit her job. She and her boss got into an argument. I suggested she try to work it out with him, and after that, she didn't leave.

Mother gave me useful advice, viewpoints, and helped me with my homework. She kept me safe without being overprotective. She chastised me when I was terrible. She praised me when I was extraordinary. She always loved me. She'd sacrifice anything for me, even her own life.

Dad, on the other hand, gave me no real affection—ever. He was my first male love, my first relationship with a man, and it was almost non-existent. Father occasionally kissed and hugged me, but every time I felt like it was more like a duty with him. I never heard him tell anyone in my family that he loved them, although I'm sure he did.

Dad lived his entire life feeling that emotion was a weakness and didn't smile much. He never admitted that any of his children were flawed. I think Dad admired me for surviving my visual challenges. But we never talked about any of this.

My father bought my affection almost every time I ran into him during several pre-college years. He was like a "Disneyland Dad," who focuses on a career, takes his little-seen child to Disney, and is elevated to fun parent status. Dad didn't take me someplace special. Instead, he put twenty-five to one hundred dollars in my hand. That was a lot of money then. He said, "Here's some extra money for you. Do whatever you want with it." That's how I built my wardrobe without elevating his status at all like a Disneyland Dad.

Dad had rigid family regimes covering appearance, behavior, and language. He was a clean freak and overbearing hairsplitter. You had to shower daily. Your teeth had to be brushed. Your hair must be combed. Your dress must be neat, clean, and proper. No attire too skimpy or short. No shorts. No cuss words. And never use the word "ugly."

For an unknown reason, Dad wouldn't let me use the word ugly. I don't think anyone would call him ugly. When I was a teen, I let it slip that I knew an ugly boy. Shaking a finger at me, he snapped, "You never say someone is ugly. Nothing in this world is ugly. We live in a beautiful world. Don't use ugly ever again." "But Daaaad, there's no other way to describe it," I pleaded. Dad growled back, "There's no such thing as ugly, period." I never let that four-letter word slip out in front of Dad again.

My parents never swore. I had to be careful not to say any cuss words in front of them. I once uttered to Daddy, "To hell with it" over something. He fumed, "What did you say?" Of course, I had to apologize for my slip of the tongue.

Dad made up for his absence at home by scheduling "quality time" with the family on Sundays. He'd say to us, "Let's go for a ride in the car . . . and have hamburgers and ice cream." Who could resist that? Shelly, three, got really excited. It showed on her face and in her words and body: "Daddy's taking me out for ice cream!" She was jumping up and down.

In the late 1930s, we kids piled into the back seat of our Depression-era gray 1934 Ford four-door sedan. We were squished. Morley got the passenger side window seat, I was in the middle and Shelly sat behind Dad. Mom sat in the front seat with Dad, who drove the same kind of car in which bandits Bonnie and Clyde were killed. It had a new, strong flathead V8 engine, popular with cops and crooks.

Dad drove west of Chicago to Lake Geneva and into Indiana. After an hour, we kids were ready to stop for hamburgers and ice cream. But Dad acted very out of the ordinary. With no one around, Dad would stop the car, get out and walk around some empty property. Puzzled Morley asked, "What is Dad looking at?" Dad didn't tell us what he was doing, and we didn't dare ask. But several times during the trip, he would do the same thing. Morley and I couldn't figure out what was going on.

We soon learned that the trip wasn't for the family to spend time together and enjoy the food at all. Dad, back in the plumbing business, was scouting property to buy to start a home-building company. Morley didn't know he'd later work for Dad and scout property himself.

Every Sunday for three years, we suffered for eight hours in the car, riding around the tri-state area just for hamburgers and ice cream. We hated these stifling weekly trips. They were so dull. We were afraid to tell Dad that. Dad wasn't any fun! All-day in the car is a long time for restless young kids like us. It was actually punishing. But we got through it by entertaining ourselves.

We couldn't wait until we got to the hilly, rolling country roads in Indiana. We singsonged in unison, "We'd go up the hill and down the hill . . . We'd go up the hill and down the hill, here we go again . . . " Even preschooler Shelly would mimic us. Such fun. From the front seat, we'd hear Dad's gruff order, "Would you be quiet in the back seat . . . ?" He didn't say, "Please."

Dad hated driving distractions. Of course, he had firm backseat instructions for us: no roughhousing and no loud talking or noises. He hated us disturbing any conversation he was having with Mom. We'd whisper jokes and stories. If we were going to laugh, we'd cover our mouths. Dad often told us, "Keep it down."

When Dad left the car to look at a property, we rough-housed until he got back. Morley would give me a punch, and Shelly asked a question to get our attention. We were creative kids and had a ball quietly playing car games. We played I Spy ("Who spies a red car?") and the Alphabet Game ("What do you see beginning with the letter A?"). We made up games to amuse ourselves, such as "Do you know anything that starts with 'B' that's a bug?"

Near the Lake Geneva Hotel in Wisconsin, I spotted signs that said, "Restricted" and "No Jews Allowed." I asked Dad, "What do those mean?" He told us about discrimination signs, widespread from 1890. Dad and I both felt that all people should be treated equally.

Finally, we got to stop and eat. We kids gobbled several square hamburgers on Chicago's South Side at White Castle, the first American fast-food chain. But my favorite get-out-of-the car stop was at an Indiana ice cream parlor. They served huge ice cream cones.

Those trips brought out the real Jekyll and Hyde character of Dad. One side of his personality was evil. He was stern in the car, curbing my emotions. His other side was good, treating us to hamburgers and ice cream. Besides perfection, Dad taught me how to get through tough times. Dad, sounding like Mom, assured me, "Nothing that happens to you in this world is so bad that you can't get through it. Whether it's sickness or a disappointment, you can overcome it."

I inherited Dad's verbal skills, such as being clear, speaking with confidence, and being concise. I saw him make speeches—I was delighted with him—and I became good at giving speeches. I had a way with words and was on the high school debating team. Dad showed me social interaction skills, including listening with understanding and empathy. I've used them to keep Naomi and my granddaughters, Amanda, Kaylee, and Chloe, close.

My sister sometimes cracked me up or pissed me off. I loved her, mothered and nurtured her from a baby. Mom didn't have time or patience to do it. Shelly was accidentally funny. In second grade, she explained that she didn't pay attention to Mom and bathe before her school picture. She said innocently, "The picture was not in color!"

CHAPTER 5 My Family, Myself

Shelly and I were awfully close. But I was hard on her sometimes. Shelly and I typically shared a bedroom. In the early 1940s, our family moved again in Uptown to a three-bedroom, two-bath apartment. This time we girls got a large bedroom with a big closet. I was neat. Shelly was messy. I was about sixteen. She was about ten.

My twin bed was neat and made. Hers was rumpled. My side of the closet had clothes neatly on hangers. Her side was helter-skelter, with clothes on the floor. I've lived to a ripe, beautiful age being tidy and quiet.

One day, I put my foot down with sis. I was so disgusted with her messiness, I divided our room in half with string. I warned her: "Shelly, you better keep your stuff on your side of the room, and if I find them on my side, I'm going to throw them out!" Mom laughed at me, laying down the law to my sister. Mom said she didn't blame me.

Our whole family was neat and clean, except Shelly was a slob. She did much better after I admonished her. I think what I said stuck with Shelly as she matured. After she married, she had six kids and her own house that was immaculate and clean.

By the early 1940s, I discovered I wouldn't get the conventional family that I expected. For several years, I had high hopes that could come true. But it didn't. I had a supportive Mom; Dad, my emotionless papa; Morley, a wise brother; and Shelly, who I nurtured. All was not lost, though. I found what it would take to change my life. It came from a choice I made that I thought I'd never do. I discovered how to enjoy the ups and downs of life wherever it took me, no matter the price I had to pay.

It all started when Mom asked, "Faith, what do you want for your tenth birthday?" I declared, "I want to go to Riverview." Riverview Park at Belmont and Western avenues in Chicago was once the "world's largest amusement park." "Faith, you can have whatever you want," Mom said. I got to go to Riverview with Mom and Morley, thirteen.

Morley begged to go on the roller coaster, named The Bobs, reputed to be the finest roller coaster of all time. I heard The Bobs distinctive, thunderous roar as we entered the park. I got some cotton candy right away. Mom wouldn't let Morley go on the ride alone. As we walked past the enticing smell of deep-frying funnel cakes, Morley begged, "Faith, will you go on it with me?" I said, "Sure." I thought Mom would say "No" and get me out of it. She didn't. Frankly, I didn't know what a roller coaster really was. But I knew it would be the most exciting birthday I ever had.

Waiting to get on the massive wooden roller coaster, I heard the passengers high above screaming for their lives, and I smelled the odor of the motors' grease and oil. I got scared. I felt like hiding. But Morley had his hand on my shoulder as I finished the candy, and I couldn't get away from him. I had butterflies of nervousness. Morley saw my face turning ashen, and assured me, "Faith, don't be scared. This will be a lot of fun." "Yeah, fun," I replied, lowering my voice to a whisper. Soon, Morley and I were tightly strapped in our sweat-stained seats. And I was still worrying.

The car started forward . . . click click click. The click-clack of the train ascending a towering lift hill produced a rush of adrenaline and anxiety all over my body. My hands tighten on the safety bar, my breath bursting in and out. Click click click. Our car went up a steep track towards a high point at eighty-seven feet. I had never been that high. I thought to myself, "Why did I let Morley take me on this ride?" But, of course, it was too late to turn back.

Shooooooop. We dropped headlong at fifty miles per hour into a hair-raising dive. Aaaaaahhhhhhhhhh. Everyone was screaming. Except me. I kept silent. I closed my eyes for a few seconds. But I couldn't keep them closed. Rattle rattle. The car raced and raced down and up through tight banked turns. Whoosh! Then steep climbs, sharp descents, and up-side-downs—over and over again. I thought it would never end. Seemed like two or three full loops of the track. I thought it just went up and down ONCE.

Finally, click click click. The car came to a halt. Screeeeeech. Ka-chunk, the seat bar went up. What a relief, it was over—and I was still alive but trembling from head to toe. I stumbled out of the car and then . . . I got so sick to my stomach, I had to go home right away. That loused up my birthday that I had looked forward to. I guess I shouldn't have eaten that sugary cotton candy. Or I probably should have stuck to the wildly ornate seventy-horse carousel.

Riverview's slogan was "Laugh Your Troubles Away." People did that through world wars, the Great Depression, divorces, and deaths. I swore I'd never ride the roller coaster again. But sometime later, Morley convinced me to ride it again with him. I was happy I did. It wasn't as bad the second time as I thought it was going to be. That first experience frightened me, weakened me, and gave me self-doubt about my ability to cope with fun things in life.

I later realized that scary challenges strengthened my character, and I was no longer afraid of them.

I was feeling good about myself. Time to celebrate by devouring Mom's homemade meals and pastries.

CHAPTER 6:
(Un)Bonding with Food

We adopted food as the sixth member of our family. Mom was a superior chef and baker. We ate Mom's delicious homemade food that often took hours to fix.

Our dinners had extraordinary powers. They brought our family together, built relationships, solved problems, and sparked celebrations.

Preparing and eating delicious food together is the best way a family can relate to each other. The food was good, but we gathered for the connections.

I loved anything Mom cooked. Some favorite foods were steak and turkey. Crave them today too. Oh, and sweets. I always loved anything sugary. What was my very favorite food? No, not cookies, ice cream, or fudge. It was apple pie. It was the food I enjoyed most while growing up—and it's still my favored food.

PART 2 WAS DAD A BAD SEED?

Mom made her own recipes for coffee cake, cinnamon rolls, cookies, and desserts. The house smelled delicious. No matter where you went, you could smell the mouth-watering scent coming from Mom's kitchen. I remember the pungent smells of apples and cinnamon of sweet apple pie.

Every time I think of apple pie today, I time travel back to my childhood three-quarters of a century ago. Apple pie is the symbol of Americana and our food culture. World War II soldiers believed they were fighting for "Mom and apple pie." That created the expression, "As American as Mom and apple pie." Funny thing is apple pie is not all that American. The apples and pie did not originally come from America. The first recorded apple pie recipe was written in England.

In our home, apple pie just wasn't dessert. It was sacred. It had enchanting power. Apple pie just brought out a rash of feelings and memories in me. The kind I got at Thanksgiving: Mom and apple pie. A pie cooling on the windowsill. Warmth. Love. Family. It's no wonder that everyone loves good old-fashioned apple pie. It sparks happy memories in me.

Besides being darn good, Mom's apple pie lifted my mood, relieved stress and anxiety, and increased my comfort. I couldn't wait for Mom to slide a slice of pie under my nose on the table. Just the thought of it quickly filled my mouth with saliva. I repeatedly swallowed, remembering how the food tasted. It evoked warm memories—momma and grandmas, windowsills, the coziness of love and family, and feelings of security and safety. I couldn't wait to dig in. Happy days were here again.

I can capture my apple pie experience by my senses. The distinct scents of caramelized apples, baking butter, cinnamon, nutmeg, and lemon juice. When Mom's pie was ready, it talked to her. As she removed it from the oven, the pie spoke out of its vents. The pie was subtlety saying, "Sizzle-sizzle-womp . . . sizzle-sizzle-womp." Sometimes it was, "Sizzle-sizzle . . . sizzle-sizzle," with no womps. I put my ear close to the pie, and I could hear it talking. It sounded very happy.

It was a great looking pie. Wow. Awww. Although I didn't have full eyesight, I could still see the golden-brown crust, with clumps of crystallized sugar. I could imagine the juicy apples piled on top of each other under the crust. Sweet, little apply-y ooze stuff flowed out of the vents, rolled down the crust, and dried. This meant there was goodness in the pie that couldn't wait to get out.

The crust was as crunchy as a thick hard pretzel, so crisp that it distinctly burst as you eased your fork into it. Granules of cinnamon hopped off the surface as it snapped. The bottom crust was golden brown, flaky, and softer than the top. A tangled string of dough joined the top and bottom crusts, saturated with ample apple filling that tasted chewy. Wrapped cozily between the crusts was a selection of crispy Granny Smiths, smothered in sweetened juice. A bite of pie melted on my tongue like butter.

This was not like one of those sugary grocery store pies. From the very first bite of Mom's pie, I got the aftertaste of apple, not sugar. When I finished my pie, I'd asked and got seconds. After that was gone, I'd cleaned my plate. I'd pick up every last crumb or apple ooze on the plate. Then I'd sit quietly for a moment, stuffed, and reflecting on how enjoyable it was.

Mom's secret touch: She added chunks of butter on top of the apples before putting the crust on. She told me she always bought the best ingredients. "Use good ingredients, and it will always come out perfect," she advised me. Here's Mom's apple pie recipe:

Mom's Perfect Old-Fashioned Apple Pie Recipe

I want to share with you Mom's Perfect Old-Fashioned Apple Pie recipe from 1938. I helped her make it as a young girl and teenager in the late '30s and early '40s. This apple pie was my favorite food that she made—cinnamony and not overly sweet. Mom's old-recipe pie tastes special. I know it contains kindness, love, and the experience of old age. And, of course, of all the apple pie recipes you can find, this one is truly perfect. Dad would accept nothing less than perfect.

Serves: 8
Total Time: Prep: 45 minutes. Bake: 45-50 minutes.

Ingredients

Filling

- ½ cup of sugar
- ½ cup packed dark brown sugar
- 3 tablespoons all-purpose flour
- 1 to 1 ½ teaspoon ground cinnamon
- 1/4 teaspoon ground nutmeg (optional)
- 1/8 teaspoon salt
- 6 to 8 thinly sliced medium apples (1 or 2 kinds: Granny Smith, Macintosh, or Jonathan)
- 2 to 4 tablespoons butter
- 1 tablespoon lemon juice

Double Crust (9 inches)

- 2 cups all-purpose flour
- ½ to 1 teaspoon salt
- ¾ cup chilled Crisco All Purpose Shortening
- 4 to 8 tablespoons ice-cold water

Directions

1. Blend all filling ingredients and set aside.

2. In a medium bowl, blend flour and salt.

3. Cut shortening into flour: Pull 2 table knives in the opposite directions.

4. Add water by the tablespoon until it resembles coarse crumbs with some small pea-sized pieces remaining. Add more water until the dough holds together when pressed.

5. Shape dough into a ball. Divide it roughly in half, making one part a little larger for the bottom crust.

6. Pre-heat oven to 425 degrees.

7. Chill the dough for 20 minutes; roll each part with a rolling pin.

8. Put the bottom crust into a 9-in. pie plate; trim dough even with edge. Lightly sprinkle flour on the dough (Mom's special touch).

9. Add the apple filling; dot with butter. Cover with top crust dough. Trim, seal, flute edges, cut slits in the center of pastry. Cover edges loosely with foil.

10. Bake 30 minutes at 425°. Remove foil. Bake another 15 to 20 minutes or until crust is brown and juice bubbles through crust slits.

11. Place on pie rack to cool. Makes 8 servings. Serve warm and add ice cream or cheddar cheese if desired.

The best thing I learned from Mom was how to cook with skill. Mom passed that on to me, starting when I was a toddler. Mom taught me how to use knives safely, searing meat, sautéing, and many other skills every cook should know. They included chopping an onion, boiling an egg, making the batter, and cooking chicken.

I passed these skills I learned from Mom on to my daughter, starting at age three. One of the first lessons was how to make chopped liver in a grinder. Naomi and I cooked quite a bit together. She's now a fabulous cook. Her prime rib today is unbelievable. In turn, Naomi taught her children cooking skills early, too, and they're fantastic in the kitchen.

Many people have forgotten about real cooking or never learned it. They rely on convenience foods, buying pre-cut vegetables, and prepared food or ordering take-out. Can you believe some people have never cooked an egg?

One of the best ways for a mother and daughter to connect is to cook together. It's such a homey-comfortable time. I looked forward to baking with my Mom. I have many fond memories of Mom and I working in the kitchen. I loved the smells of the baked pies, cookies, and also mashed potatoes. I wanted my daughter and her children to have those too.

I don't cook much anymore. Naomi is always afraid I won't have enough food. A food packaging executive, she comes to see me every few months. She cooks delicious food for me and packs my refrigerator and freezer with them. I've got lamb chops, prime rib, pizza (from scratch), chicken-vegetable soup, and much more. The fridge's so full I can't find anything. One of my hardest decisions every day is what to eat for dinner. Tonight, I think I'll warm her cooked prime rib (it's the best) and add mashed potatoes and a vegetable salad.

I remember once Mom had just baked an apple pie and put it on the windowsill to cool. I was young, don't know how old, and I climbed up on the windowsill to see some birds fighting outside. I loved to climb. I accidentally stepped in the middle of a gorgeous, nine-inch apple pie that Mom planned to serve at dinner. I heard my dirty shoe make a soft squishing sound like I was splashing through soft mud. "Wha, whaaa."

I started crying, and Mom rushed into the kitchen. I sniveled, "Mom, don't hate me. I didn't mean to do it." She forgave me. Not only did I give Mom dirty dough, but I gave her a fully cooked, dirty apple pie. I said, "Mom, I'll help you bake another one."

CHAPTER 6 (Un)Bonding with Food

The one thing that brings people together is food. I think a family that cooks together stays together. It's one of the best ways to spend quality time with your children or grandchildren. The whole family can help prepare and cook and then enjoy their efforts, including babies and toddlers. Repeatedly give them kitchen safety rules. Always supervise them.

You can find excellent information on family cooking on the Internet. We didn't have the Internet then. We learned much of this on our own. Here are some ideas for kitchen jobs for all age levels:

Preschoolers can help with some simple tasks. They include sprinkling salt, pepper or seasonings onto a dish (practices a motor skill); feeling bread or dough by helping knead it (experiences a sensory event); counting eggs or other ingredients (improves counting skills); talking about recipes and ingredients (builds vocabulary); and tasting some ingredients, if they want (helps with picky eaters).

A baby or toddler in a kitchen highchair will experience many new smells. The baby will develop visual tracking, watching you move around. If you explain what you are doing, baby communication skills develop.

School-aged kids can be more responsible in the kitchen. They may help crack eggs, stir a stovetop sauce with your supervision, peel potatoes or apples with safe peelers, use a rolling pin, and help make a shopping list. When you feel a child can safely cut and dice, give him or her thorough instructions and cautions. As a result, you'll boost your child's confidence, seeing the finished product enjoyed by the family. Children will also learn good eating habits and use math, science, and creativity skills. They may even appreciate meals more, knowing all the demanding work that goes into them.

I'm so thankful that I connected to my family with food. Without it, I don't know whether I could survive what was coming next.

CHAPTER 7:
Big, Screwed-Up Family

At the start of the 1940s, I couldn't wait to get back to the comfort of my Chicago home from my extraordinary adventures. I was a changed person—more seasoned and ready to take on the world.

I was ten and starting fifth grade. Dad had started a new plumbing and heating business. We were cheerful, content, and at ease with the world. This is what families are supposed to be. Full of family fun. Mom and I were riveted to our new radio, the most important means of communication then. We loved listening to soap operas. Mom made potato salad and chicken for sharing with Dad's Russian friends at a Sunday picnic.

On a sleepy Sunday morning, our family was listening to the Chicago Bears-Chicago Cardinals football game on WGN Radio. I was really dreaming about presents I wanted for Christmas, less than three weeks away. Our family was Jewish, but we always celebrated Christmas.

PART 2 WAS DAD A BAD SEED?

At about 1:30 p.m. on Dec. 7, 1941, an announcer broke into the play-by-play account: "Flash—White House says Japs attack Pearl Harbor!" The Japanese surprise attack on our Pearl Harbor naval base drew the U.S. into World War II. The turbulent Stormy Forties was the darkest time of my life. Our country and my family sank to the brink of disaster.

Mom, sitting right next to the radio, knew it was catastrophic, sobbing, "All our sailors and soldiers killed over there . . . " Up until then, the radio made us laugh with comedy shows like *Amos 'n' Andy*. Now it moved Mom to cry. We lost more than 2,400 men, and I was scared. The world was spinning. I was biting my lip. Uncle Shep, an Army private who was living with us, rushed back to his Illinois base but didn't fight in the war. Morley was in the Navy, but he stayed stateside too.

It was the most horrific war. Our country lost 1.3 million lives. The conflict changed America. It helped pull us out of the Depression. It ushered in the Baby Boom, the Cold War, the Affluent Society, sprawling suburbs, and the way we live today. It was the seed for McDonald's, computers, wonder drugs, and innovation. And I've lived through it all. God Bless America and its brave men and women in uniform.

I was fighting escalating battles on my home front. Somehow I outlasted catastrophes in my broken-down family. Deep into another toxic situation, I lost sleep, trying to find a way to get entirely away from my father. He worked hard and played hard and gave me no love.

We prayed for six million Jews murdered during the war and Grandpa Louis, who was killed by a streetcar. Mom stopped keeping a kosher house then, and we rejoiced. It simplified our complicated family life. Yet, I never gave up seeking a better time for me . . . and my dog.

During World War II, just about everything was scarce and rationed, especially tires, sugar, and meat. Meat rationing started buying panics, overcharges, under-the-table payments, and a widespread black market.

We had a little terrier dog named Terry. We all loved him and spoiled him. He enjoyed hamburger meat. I was sixteen, and Mom sent me to the store with a grocery list. I felt so stupid asking the butcher, "Can I have a quarter pound of cheap hamburger meat for my dog?" The burly butcher got red in the face, scowled at me, and fumed, "Don't you know there's a war going on, and meat is scarce. How can you give it to a dog? People need it."

I shyly begged, "Our dog is like a family member. It's only a quarter of a pound." When he saw my eyes tearing, he faintly groaned and gave me the meat without saying anything. Terry ate a significant portion of our family meat allowance that week. But it was worth it. I was happy I saw our dog wolfing the meat down in three or four bites, and of course, begging us with his eyes for more.

PART 2 WAS DAD A BAD SEED?

"Sorry, Terry, there's no more," I explained. "You don't know how lucky you were to get even that!" I had a big mouth and a tiny brain. I could have made other butcher shop customers mad. Or I might have gotten into trouble with the federal government.

I soothed my sorrow eating fudge and malts.

The government rationed the main ingredient of ice cream, sugar, but fortunately, my local drugstore never ran out of confections. General Eisenhower made sure our troops got plenty of milkshakes and ice cream. I think ice cream gave our soldiers enough moral support to help win the war for the Allies against Germany. Sweets have always relieved my hurt. As an adult, they put me in touch with my inner child. If I'm upset, I'll eat chocolate as comfort food. It offers solace and makes me feel good.

Walking home after high school classes, Ettie and I and a couple other girls would all buy fudge at one of the best bakeries in town, Davidson's at Broadway and Argyle. I frequently bought the biggest piece of fudge they had— a four-inch square two inches thick, as large as a side plate. I'd nibble on it while walking home.

It had the heavenly tang of sweet, good chocolate fresh from the pan. My fingers felt its lingering warmth. My mouth was drooling uncontrollably as my teeth squished gently into that rich morsel. My taste buds woke up, releasing the full fudge flavor on my tongue. Those blissful moments filled my tummy and soothed my nerves.

CHAPTER 7 Big, Screwed-Up Family

My friends and I hung out at the soda fountain at the corner drugstore, Markus Drugs, a short walk from home past fancy houses. It was in the Uptown neighborhood on Chicago's North Side, close to Lake Michigan and wide sandy beaches.

Frank Sinatra got his break in Uptown at the Aragon Ballroom, and the film industry started there before it moved to Hollywood. The soda fountain was the neighborhood meeting place. Over sodas, sundaes, and milkshakes, us kids, as well as adults, enjoyed friendly conversation and lots of laughs. We'd giggle over young lovers in the corner, sipping a malt with two straws.

I remember the drugstores back then as impressive from the second I opened the door. I breathed its romantic smell—vanilla, cologne, and the pure medicinal pharmaceuticals of what was my second home. It was happy times, unlike what prevailed at home. Street corner drugstore soda fountains, like Markus, were neat. They were lined with fun display cases with stained-glass trim, decorated with mahogany woodwork everywhere and real tile floors. At the shiny marble countertop, they had fixed swivel stools. They were complemented by little, round tables and rounded wire-back chairs and wood booths along the walls.

I wore bobbysox or anklets. My tall, boyish soda jerk made the most fabulous flavored soda water concoctions on earth—fast. His name was Tommy. He chatted with me, by name, flirted with all the girls, and we flirted back. If I ordered a strawberry shake with raspberries on top, Tommy loudly called out the order in verbal shorthand, "Shake One in the Hay and Spit on It." Soda jerks used their own jargon, adding mystique to their job. They loved putting on a show.

I often ordered a malt. I can still see Tommy slowly placing the order in front of me at the counter—and topping his service with a quick wink of the eye. Malts were served in a metal container, so you could easily have a refill. I can picture the drops of condensation on those stainless-steel canisters slowly falling to the marble counter.

My favorite sweet was chocolate fudge sundaes. The original 1881 ice cream sundae was sold only on Sundays. I'm glad they stopped just making them on Sundays. I ate them any day of the week! I'm not alone. Americans eat among the most ice cream of anyone in the world (New Zealand is first). I'm happy to do my part.

I'm surprised that I wasn't a fat kid. I was called "The Bean Pole." My teachers would write notes to my parents telling them I was too thin. They asked, "Is there food in your house?" "Is Faith eating at home?" I was always a good eater and ate reasonably sized portions of food at home. I was just a highly active person, maybe even hyperactive.

I wasn't worried about my weight. Just my daddy issues. I was naughty. I broke Dad's ground rules and took risks. If I didn't, life wouldn't be any fun. He was the strict dad, I was the sneaky kid. My best Senn High School friend was Alice. Her first-floor bedroom faced mine across a rat alley, the narrow alley between our two apartment buildings.

On weekday nights when we were supposed to be doing homework, we'd open our windows at eight or nine o'clock at night. I'd whisper to her, "Let's go to the Plantation for ribs" (best ribs in town, four or five blocks away), or she'd ask, "How about a walk on the beach?" We lived three to four blocks from a park and Foster Beach along Lake Michigan.

You might think we climbed out of our bedroom windows. No, we just quietly walked out of our front doors. We didn't have to go past our parents. They were in rooms not near the front doors. We silently got back to our bedrooms by using our house keys to get ready for school the next morning. It was a big thrill to get away with it. We snuck out three times a week for two or three hours on school nights for four years of high school. I was amazed we sneaked out more than 600 times, and our parents never caught us!

I had dreadful fears in my high school years. Not fitting in with other students, facing peer pressure to do something I didn't want to do. I was scared on my first day of high school. It was Sept. 2, 1941, at Nicholas Senn High School, a crowded 5,000-student public school in

Chicago's prestigious Edgewater lakefront section on the North Side.

My stomach was churning on the day of my official high school debut. I had the jitters. Most friends had their outfits planned for months. But not me. I wore a plain skirt, blouse and a sweater, saddle shoes, and short curly hair. I didn't even fix my hair. It was a mess.

When we got to school, I looked up at its structure with awe. It was a Classical Revival style, three-story building that spanned more than a whole city block. The school was so large, I wasn't sure I was in the right homeroom. I was lost and afraid.

I had sexual fears. That's where my brother helped me. I never had "The Talk" about sex with my old-fashioned parents. I learned about sex from my friends and Morley. I was a virgin, and Morley was the only one I could talk to about sex. I wasn't looking for it. But I think I had virginity written all over me by the way I dressed—kind of nerdy, conservative. Mom knitted most of my clothes to Dad's no-skimpy or short dress specifications.

My brother fixed me up to date a few of his boyfriends. He always reminded them, "Hey, this is my sister. She's hands-off if you want to lay her." I'd tell Morley whether my date was platonic, lustful, or tried to get me into bed. I asked Morley, "What technique do I use on guys who put hands on me? I don't like it. I'm not ready." He told me, "Just tell them that."

I was terrified of sewing. With my limited sight, I couldn't see well enough to thread a needle. I found many of my blouses and dresses were missing buttons, and I didn't remember losing them. I asked Mom, "Why are so many buttons missing?" She didn't answer. I knew she secretly removed the buttons. She said, handing me several buttons, "Here, you'll have to sew these buttons back on your blouse."

Mom regularly gave me a blouse and watched me sew the buttons on it. I had to do it by feel, rather than sight. This was Mom's button therapy, another game she created, like Find the Pennies, to help me see better. Seeing me grappling threading a needle, my preteen sister blurted out, "Let me do it for her." "No," Mom said, "she has to learn to do these things herself."

I fell in love with the violin, but I was scared of taking lessons and playing before a group of people. Dad gave me a beautiful, expensive violin. Imagine me sitting, holding the violin and bow with two hands and also holding the sheet music inches from my eyes. Couldn't be done. I couldn't see the sheet music on the music stand a couple feet away while I played the violin. I created a cheat sheet, so I could see the notes on the music stand while playing the violin. I transcribed the notes into large numbers, signifying specific notes, and put it on the stand.

My biggest fear was that someday I'd wake up completely blind. That dream terrified me. When I couldn't fall asleep, I'd visualize a world that might always be completely dark. I could lose my independence and my ability to see colors and reading. How would I do things if I couldn't see a little bit? I couldn't see the color of trees, flowers, and the sky, only black and white. I didn't know how I would ever function. I thought, Oh, dear. God, please don't make my world go away. Most blind people can see anywhere from only very bright lights to blurry images just below my legal blindness level.

Mom kept nagging me to go to the world-famous Mayo Clinic in Rochester, Minnesota, to see if they could improve my vision. I finally went and asked the doctor who examined me, "Will I ever go blind?" The doctor told me, "You're amazing. You're using your eyes to the best of your ability. You've learned to use your eyes more than many people who have come through here. Continue with what you are doing, and you'll never lose your vision. There's nothing more that we can do for you beyond what your doctors have already done."

At my high school graduation in 1945, I was happy and sad. Character Zack Morris of the TV sitcom *Saved by the Bell* said, "I thought the last day of high school would be the best day of my life until I realized what I'd be leaving."

For me, I'd be leaving the four best years of my life. I made lifelong friends, I debated on the school team and acted in a play. I had a B average. I excelled in writing poetry and barely passed algebra. At the graduation ceremony, I saw about one hundred empty seats, among the 500 graduates, reserved for boys fighting or killed in World War II. I prayed for them and their families. After my graduation milestone and World War II, everyone was trying to put their lives back together.

But I wondered what was ahead for me.

Soon, I got my last eye procedure while in college—the fifteenth by age eighteen, after I had many pairs of glasses, contact lenses, and medicines. I think Dr. Brown gave me a laser procedure on my right eye to enlarge the pupil. But I have been told since that laser eye surgery was not developed until much later. Sometime after the procedure, I was amazed at how much better I could see than before. I looked out a window and could see more detail on tree leaves and flower petals and if a person had a ring on his or her finger.

I needed a better, more stable life. And I found it. Family struggles and high school were behind me. I discovered that I was capable of guiding my future—and I took it. As I grew, I found that I could have more individuality, self-confidence, and develop my own identity. Most of all, I learned that life was still more fun if I did something naughty or went against the grain of previous ideas, beliefs, or principles. I took on a new, more promising life. I was more grown-up, more conscious, and at peace with myself.

I was ready to take on the world on my own terms.

[Page Intentionally Blank]

CHAPTER 8:
The Blind Black Sheep

Just age thirteen, I was the family outcast—the defiant, rebellious blind black sheep. People described me in many ways: Teen rebel. Maverick. Nonconformist. Wayward. Misunderstood. Rejected. The lone wolf. Didn't blend in. The scapegoat for all family problems.

Yet, I was decent. I wasn't bad, just different. I squinted. I read material close to my eyes. I dressed oddly and played like boys. I took more risks than the rest of the family. I had a unique lifestyle and values. My life revolved around my eyesight and staying out of hot water. I faced personal scraps that others did not. I felt as bad as an orphan or abandoned child, who were other misfits unable to adjust to their situations.

"I assure you, I am the black sheep of the family," wrote General George S. Sternbeater in *Bleak Expectations*. "And while that would normally make me a criminal or a lunatic, in my evil family it makes me noble and decent!" I thought that too. I stood out in my family flock like a sore thumb. I was more rascally and got into difficulty more often than my siblings.

I faced unexplored darkness in my life. That was my crisis. I examined my inner thoughts as the black sheep of the family. I was taken outward in the uncertain unknown. I was trapped in a flawed flock of white sheep. I somehow needed to shed my black sheep image and get on with my life.

When Dad came home for dinner, he had a pecking order. First, he'd say hello to Shelly, pick her up and hug her. Then Dad would greet Morley. Finally, he came to me, like an afterthought, and said only, "Hi," with usually no further conversation.

I was the unfavorite child of my family. I was given the least parental favoritism. Dad loved my siblings more than me. He put them on pedestals.

Dad revered Morley, his favorite child. Morley was the firstborn and could watch out for his siblings. Dad and Morley had a unique father-son relationship. Full of pride, Dad groomed Morley to run his home-building business. Morley became president of one of Dad's sister home-building companies. After that, he was assistant regional administrator of the federal Occupational Safety and Health Administration. Morley closed his career as head of his own Evanston, Illinois engineering consulting company. He died at age eighty-seven.

Chapter 8 The Blind Black Sheep

Dad gave Shelly more affection than me. He fell all over his little girl, the youngest child. Dad often played up his admiration for her. He'd often ask her, "How's my baby." If Morley and I bullied her, Dad sent us to our rooms. When I saw Dad pick up Shelly and cuddle her, I just felt I had to work harder to earn his recognition.

Growing up, Shelly and I fought the glorious war of sister rivalry. We competed for pretty much everything — love, attention, food, and who gets the only bathroom first. This helped build my character and skills and defined my place in the world. Dad made sure Shelly won the war, so I was bound to become the unfavorite. Things between us sisters didn't really get horrible. We knew each other well enough, though, to understand the hateful things that would hurt the other the most. Shelly became a bank executive, had six children by age thirty, and lives near me in Florida now.

I was the overlooked middle child, and very rarely are they the family favorite. By birth order, I became the unfavorite almost automatically.

Dad was icy and aloof with me. He never told me eye-to-eye he loved me. All I wanted from him was his love. Blindness disgusted him. Dad never recognized my success. I played and learned like every kid. He always compared me to his superior child: "Honestly, Faith, why can't you be more like Morley."

PART 2 WAS DAD A BAD SEED?

My father could be blunt, cruel, and insulting, especially to me. But colleagues and even strangers never forgot him. They were captivated by his gift for gab. Dad was a conversationalist. You knew he was present, and he would talk to anybody about anything, especially building construction. He loved engaging people in conversation.

I thought he was very handsome, except for his bulbous nose. He was short, about 5 feet, 8 inches, and overweight at 178 pounds. His round face was dark, his eyes brown, and his hair was thick and black. In his sixties, his hair started turning white. He often wore a light-colored Fedora hat with a dark band. Hats were a required fashion for men until the 1960s.

Dad was never full of fun or gloom. In fact, he was dull. Dad was very straight-laced. Straightforward ("Do as I say"). Not a story or joke teller. A smiler with a little sense of humor, but rarely laughed. Not an athlete or hobbyist. Physically active, but I never saw him carry anything heavy.

I tussled with my increasingly egocentric, psychopathic dad. He had many traits of the personality disorder called psychopathy, affecting about 1 percent of Americans. Psychopaths often show a combination of charm and emotionlessness. They basically lack empathy, are manipulative, irresponsible, and will violate people's rights. Many are successful citizens. Some are coldblooded killers. They blend into the population. The average person walks by seven psychopaths a day! They could be a friend—or a dad.

I don't know how I got such a defective Dad. He had a lot of bad traits. They were: antisocial behavior, lack of ability to love, little remorse and empathy, indifference, and failure to learn from experiences. Others were lying, lack of guilt, cunning and manipulative, superficial charm, shallow emotional response, sexual promiscuity, and criminal tendencies.

I finally figured out my black sheep situation. I miserably stayed in my family flock, as sheep do to graze together. The sheep don't particularly like each other. But they stick close for protection and follow each other around. While eating grass and shrubs, they can only survive danger by running from it. I stayed close to my family as sheep do. But now a threat was mounting, and stakes were rising. I fought to solve dire straits within my family.

One of the hardest emotions I faced was the pain and agony of being a black sheep. Lots of emotional distress and rejection to cope with and heal. I searched to "find the gold in the mud." Trying to understand feelings of rejections . . . Questioning my sanity . . . Scorn and alienation took a toll on me—continually standing up for myself and trying to fit in. I took on much guilt and stress for being exceptional.

PART 2 WAS DAD A BAD SEED?

I never wanted to be rejected again. I kept people at arm's length and closed my heart to other people. But then I longed to have healthy, close romantic relationships with men. I wanted intimacy but feared getting it and sabotaged the idea.

Father was hardly home, found a mistress, had a child out of wedlock, divorced Mom (trying to get over a miscarriage), and abandoned us kids.

I'm sure Mom fulfilled Dad's sexual needs. But Dad couldn't get enough sex. He just had a libido that made him have to have more. Dad led a secret life. Many family members didn't know. Throughout his adult life, he was a playboy. He was a rake, a sexually unrestrained person who had sunk below usual moral standards. I felt sorry for Mom. She gave her love to a man who didn't know how to really give it back to her.

I deserved a healthy family that would completely support me no matter what. But we were a mixed-up and fragile family, horribly bleak with weighty relationship problems. A vital sign that we had a dysfunctional family was father's inflexible rules.

Dad had to be superb at whatever he did. He always dressed smartly. No matter what he wore—suit or sports clothes. Dad insisted that Mom clean all his clothes, so he looked impeccable every day. Dad wanted his kids to look immaculate too. Dad appeared perfect on the outside but was deeply imperfect inside.

Chapter 8 The Blind Black Sheep

He gave me the disgraceful black sheep complex. He thought I was a failure among his kids because I had a sight impairment. Morley and Shelly were flawlessly healthy. Dad never told me to my face that I was the family's black sheep. This is not unusual in families. It was a subtle feeling, with nothing said directly about it. But he certainly made me feel that I was the odd one out. I sensed it in the back of my mind, felt it in my heart, and disregarded it with a smile on my face.

Dad took me for granted. He never talked about my eyes to me or even routinely asked me how I was doing. He never read to me like Mom did or even took me for an ice cream cone, just father and daughter.

I failed at being a regular child. Dad made me abnormal through tight control and manipulation. As novelist Carson McCullers wrote," The hearts of small children are delicate organs. A cruel beginning in this world can twist them into curious shapes."

In my family, people often didn't pay attention to each other. This is a fundamental characteristic of an impaired family.

Father put incredible pressure on me, not just to do my best but to do the impossible, such as quickly reading small print. Being whole was impossible for me. He took the child playfulness out of me and made it harder for me to learn. My self-esteem suffered, making me feel incompetent and worthless. I lived much of my childhood trying to appease my strict, excessively domineering Dad rather than becoming the best person I could be.

I fit the definitions of a black sheep. I stuck out from the rest of the family. I didn't follow Dad's unyielding family rulebook. I was a scapegoat, causing all my family's problems. A black sheep "causes shame or embarrassment because of deviation from the accepted standards of his or her group." Or a black sheep "(is) a member of a family or group who is regarded as a disgrace to them." Shepherds first used the term black sheep to describe an occasional black sheep born into a flock of all-white sheep. Black wool was less valuable than white wool.

I believed Morley may have felt uncomfortable, ashamed, or angry about my eye condition or black sheep status. He just didn't admit it. He and I were in high school at the same time. When I was a freshman, Morley was a senior. He told me he'd watch over me. But Morley asked me not to tell anyone he was my big brother. He whispered to me in school, "Don't ask my friends or me for directions to classes. You're on your own. I want you to stand on your own two feet."

I can't entirely blame Dad for the way he was. He had a rough childhood himself, which shaped his adult behavior. Dad became his family's breadwinner at age fourteen, took care of his mom and siblings, and probably never really enjoyed his childhood. As a result, he became an over-disciplined fusspot. He brought his socially impaired youth into my life. Dad never changed, and I suffered.

Through tenacity, I discovered what would alter my life completely. I overcame the blind sheep crisis by distancing myself from Dad. I found my own small group of friends—a new flock of black sheep. They were unusual black sheep of their own families. They became my real family and faithful friends.

Dad always told the family, "Blood is thicker than water." At first, I didn't know what Dad meant. It's a proverb that says family bonds (blood relations) are more important than temporary relationships with friends. Mafia members used the phrase to remind each other that their loyalty to the family was all that matters.

But I found blood is not thicker than resonance. Family is not more important than my friends. They resonate with me because we are alike or compatible. Clarissa Pinkola Estés, Ph.D., author of *The New York Times* bestseller, *Women Who Run With the Wolves: Myths and Stories of the Wild Woman Archetype,* wrote: "Find those you truly belong to. Blood is not thicker than resonance..." Estés quotes poet Charles Simic, "He who cannot howl, will not find his pack."

I howled and found my pack, a black sheep flock of like-minded friends. Now I was living the life I wanted to live. Wasn't trying to live by Dad's rules. This set me free to be me, a life advancing experience. Still, a black sheep, though. Once a black sheep, always a black sheep.

I was happy to be the black sheep. It opened new doors for me. It gave me hidden power that other family members did not have. I accepted my particular imperfections and characteristics as part of my journey in life. I wear my black sheep label with honor. There are good things about it. I wanted to heal, so I took the hidden power of being a black sheep. My life would never be the same again.

The Black Sheep archetype produced emotional pain and covert power for me. But it also gave me an influence advantage over my siblings. As a black sheep, I found:

- More freedom to explore the world and find a better home.
- More opportunity to develop the life I genuinely wanted, including work, dress, worship, and love.
- A greater sense of self and individuality than other family members. The black sheep may have more psychological scars than more accepted family members.
- More opportunities to empathize with other people in society and the world.
- Opportunity to locate my "wolf pack" friends that I more closely identify with than my family. They can love and cherish me in ways my family cannot do.

I was happy as the black sheep of my new family. . . . until the next life challenge that I didn't know whether I'd ever get through.

CHAPTER 9:
Fire and Ice

Strangely, I was comfortable as the black sheep in two families by age fifteen. In my natural family, Shelly and I giggled about Mom giving us a baby sister or brother soon. In my new high school family of friends, I confessed that I kissed Tommy last night.

Mom and Dad had a relationship that became icy. Dad and his personal office secretary, Fran, had one that was on fire. Mom was a little dull and sweet. Fran was edgy and a bitch. I needed Mom and Dad back together for the family to stay close. Our family was already volatile. What more could we bear? I did not solve the crisis. Unfortunately, our family problems got worse every day.

Mother was a fantastic Jewish cook. No one would want to miss a meal of hers . . . except for Dad. Mom knew damn well that Dad was messing around with his mistress. He preached family togetherness to us. Yet, Dad had a lying, cheating heart. Love makes your heart go pitter-patter, but love can leave you heartbroken.

Now, instead of food uniting my family, it split us up when Dad was absent.

Mom had a stillbirth in the middle of World War II. Dad badly wanted another child, and Mom couldn't give it to him. I took the stillbirth extremely hard. Mom let Shelly, nine, and me, fifteen, name the expectant baby before the delivery. If the baby were a girl, we'd call her Linda.

Shelly and I just finished changing the covers on the six dining room chairs. Mom, wearing a formal navy-blue suit, supervised us. Around the house, she always wore an elegant, chic dress, not traditional dresses and never pants or house dresses. Mom stood and announced, "Uh-oh, something's wrong. The baby isn't moving!" Mom rushed to the hospital in a cab. We found out the umbilical cord strangled the baby. Mom had a history of miscarriages and abortions, and this was probably her last chance to give birth.

When she came home from the hospital, she asked Shelly and me to return the layette to the children's store where she bought it. Mom packed it with diapers, clothing, and bedding. It was so heavy, Shelly and I carried it with each of us on an end. As we left the house, hurtful tears streamed down our faces. People looked at us as we stepped purposely and haltingly to the store, as in a funeral procession.

We both walked into the store with blurred vision. A saleslady looked at us sorrowfully. We didn't say anything. She immediately knew what happened. She took the layette from us, didn't say a word, and handed us twenty-three dollars back.

At school the next day, I broke down at my desk when I heard the music the teacher was playing. It was *Pavane for a Dead Princess* by French composer Maurice Ravel. It's about a little princess (infanta). Such a beautiful piece. Such an unhappy time for me. But baby Linda still lives in our family. Ten years afterward, Shelly named her first daughter Linda in memory of the original Linda.

Meanwhile, gossiping old ladies in our neighborhood were appalled that Dad slept with his attractive, auburn-haired secretary, twelve years his junior. Back then, marriage was permanent, divorce uncommon, and an affair was scandalous. Dad's mistress was Frances Novak, a childless widow of a machinist who died a few years earlier. She was born as Mary Ann Lulek in Pennsylvania to needy Catholic Hungarian-Polish parents of four children and did not go to high school. Mary Ann changed her name to Frances and suspiciously used several name variations in public records.

Fran mate-poached Dad. He could give her the money and comforts she never had in life. Fran was the vulture, and Joe was her prey. She swooped in on Dad when Mom was most vulnerable with a stillbirth. Fran was a gold digger who found an older sugar daddy and mooched off his money and booming home-building status in exchange for sex.

Somehow the seductress may have conned Dad out of his fortune a decade before he died. She was a bitch (wolf) in sheep's clothing—outwardly innocent but ruthless inside in getting Dad's money. She may have killed Dad emotionally for his money.

I think Fran became enamored with Dad for a couple reasons. Dad would boost her narcissistic ego. She probably thought, "If I can pry him away from his wife and kids, then I must be someone exceptional and extraordinary." She also thought Dad would make a great father of her children. He was time-tested with three of his own.

Dad played Mom for a sucker. Their marriage was on the rocks. Dad continued to play the part of a hard-working wage earner. He expected Mom to continue being his faithful wife, cooking, cleaning the house, and raising the kids. Dad paid attention to Mom, making her feel happier and getting her pregnant at age thirty-six.

In 1943, he realized their marriage was over after more than twenty-two years. The next year Fran gave him a baby, though illegitimate. My new half-brother was named Robert, who we called Bob or Bobby. We think Dad was the father, but we're not sure.

Chapter 9 Fire and Ice

Before Bobby's birth, I was facing the most challenging part of my young life. I was no longer a kid, but not quite an adult. I had reached the bittersweet seventeen.

This was a coming of age when I made the mental leap from a child to an adult. And from learning high school algebra to discovering the dark side of adultery, illicit children, and divorce. I just wondered if my transition would turn out all right.

Dad loved the idea of having a young, glamorous, auburn-haired sexpot draped over his shoulders. He wanted a sensual cheerleader who turned him on. He thought Fran would give him more satisfying sex, more children, and more extensive power and status. She was with his business from the beginning, always meticulously dressed in dark business suits that showed off her lovely figure. Never a hair out of place, even on her own time at the pool.

Fran was a smooth vamp, who charmed, attracted, and exploited Dad. With her persuasive charm and enticing looks, she could quickly wrap any man around her little finger. And Dad could charm the panties off any woman without even trying. An unexpected chick magnet, Dad attracted vulnerable women at the drop of his hat. Like a Hollywood script, they each fed their egos and got the thrill of being in bed together.

I got the shock of my life in 1945! I was eighteen and was just starting my freshman year at Indiana University. I was alone studying at my desk in the dorm when Mom called. She told me that she and my father were getting divorced—and asked if Shelly could visit me. I felt heartsick for my mother, thinking, "I don't understand how Dad could do that to her." The divorce was about a year after Bobby's birth. I wondered why they waited so long.

When twelve-year-old Shelly learned of our parents' divorce, she pondered, "Daddy's not coming home anymore?" She was inconsolable when she visited me at college. I calmed her: "What Mom and Dad do is their lives. You've got your life to worry about. We can't control other people." As we commiserated together, we bonded more intensely during the crisis.

My parents never talked to me about divorce. Dad couldn't look me in the eyes after the breakup. Mom told us kids, "Always respect your father and try to visit him as much as you can." We had lunch with Dad regularly and occasionally visited him in his new home in the now ritzy Chicago suburb of Wilmette.

After the divorce, Mom didn't want to go to any more family gatherings and wasn't even invited. She never again saw Dad, the only man Mom ever loved. Mother became unhappy, lonely, and depressed for a while. She had no faith in her future or with men. She dated a few men. But she quickly soured on the idea. After Dad, Mom never loved again. She told me, "I'm swearing off men—for good!" Over the next half-century, she lived with Shelly and me and her sister Belle at various times. She died at age eighty-eight, with Joe in her memory and alone.

Six months after my parents divorced, Dad, forty-four, married Fran, thirty-two, in Chicago. In addition to Bob, they had two more boys, William (Billy) and Michael (Mike). But Dad never gave up being a playboy. I thought he was happy with Fran. But Dad's sexual drive got the best of him. He wined and dined women at his post-divorce, luxury, suburban homes north of Chicago from the mid-1940s into the '60s. He had three large homes in Mount Prospect, in Wilmette (Canterbury mansion off Lake Michigan), and in the Village of Kildeer (Long Grove Farms).

In my opinion, Fran turned out to be a wicked step-mom or step-monster. She had always pampered herself and bought expensive clothing and cosmetics. But now she was like the Queen in Snow White. "If there's anything fairy tales have taught us, it's that first wives are perfect, and second wives are horrible," said Bart in *The Simpsons*. Bow down to Queen Fran! I saw that she sat on her throne and pathetically ordered her family around like servants. When she wanted a drink, she'd call to Mike or Bob to get one, and they would come running.

A prima donna, she wasn't a housewife. I never saw her in the kitchen, and she snubbed dirtying her hands. Nor did she mess with raising her three children. She always had a maid do that.

PART 2 WAS DAD A BAD SEED?

I believe she pretended to love her stepchildren. Fran was overly friendly with me and turned on her compelling charm to win us cautious stepkids over. I never forgave her for stealing Dad. But she gave me expensive slacks and a top and other gifts. Fran always invited me over to their house, helped me pick my wedding dress and trousseau (Dad paid), and plan the wedding. We became good friends. Yet, she was my friendly enemy. We kids, though, were angry and resentful over the divorce. I detested her, behaving like she's my mother. I wanted to say to her, "I know my mom, and Fran, you're no Bessie Brickman!"

Fran seemed jealous of our relationship with Dad. This is the most taboo emotion a stepmother can have. It fits the cliché of the green-eyed step-monster. Fran was green with envy. As a result, Dad's first and second families were irreversibly separated, but we still got together at "family disunions." After the divorce, Dad spent little time with his first family and me. Dad and Fran would only have us over for Christmas dinner and special occasions.

My stepmom prevented me from seeing my dying dad. She wouldn't let anyone in his first family see him on his death bed. When I asked Fran, the second-family matriarch, if I could see him in the hospital, she gave this excuse, "Well, not today. He's too sick. He might not even know you." I shouted back, "I don't care if he knows me or not, I want to see my father." He was suffering from brain cancer, but this is not what Dad would have wanted. He wanted his first family to see each other often. I never got to see him before he passed.

Even when a black sheep leaves home, she is still blamed for family problems in absentia.

Maybe that's why Dad or his second wife wouldn't see me. He or she may have blamed me for causing his disease. He might have distanced himself from his first family for his own mental well-being. Even on Dad's death bed, thirty years after divorcing our family, I was still the ostracized child. This is common. I was again abused mentally. I was turned away when asking to say goodbye to Dad, unable to ever escape the black sheep role he gave me.

If I visited Dad, I believe Fran was afraid we might find out that Dad's first family would get nothing in his will. When Dad last talked to us three kids, he assured us, "You'll be provided for in my will when I die." Dad always intended to take care of his first family, Bessie and us three kids. Many years before Dad's death, he supposedly gave Morley 20 percent interest in the family business. Dad gave Shelly a big house.

A decade before his death, Dad gave me a twenty-or-thirty-thousand dollar, three-bedroom townhouse in Evanston after I got married. But George and I had to pay the mortgage! Dad promised to leave me something in his will. But I got nothing, nor did Mom or my siblings. I really didn't want his dirty money. But he promised it to me.

PART 2 WAS DAD A BAD SEED?

I didn't want to be beholden to him, even if he was dead. I think Fran finagled Dad's million-dollar estate for herself and perhaps her three sons. I was expecting a substantial inheritance. But Fran bought my friendship and stole my birthright.

After Dad passed, Fran continued to live in luxury. She stayed in their three-bedroom, four-and-a-half-bath ranch home in the affluent Lake Michigan Chicago suburb of Lake Forest. From what I know of her, she must have lived high on the hog. She liked the best crystal and silver, expensive house furnishings, top-of-the-line designer clothes, wrinkle-preventing cucumber facials, and more bathrooms than bedrooms!

Suffering from Alzheimer's, Frances A. Brickman died in Lake Forest in 2007 at age ninety-four, thirty years after Dad died. My half-brother Michael is the only living son of Dad. He and his wife own the luxurious forty-acre Long Grove Farms riding barn and stable in Kildeer.

Dad seemed like two different people—the rake and the wise, loving father. Dad believed that healthy family relationships are the most important thing you can ever have in life. "Put love of family first," he told us.

That was good advice. We kids vowed that we would stay chummy no matter what, even if anyone of us louses something   up.

CHAPTER 10:
Messing Up Life

"Why do you stand up to me, Faith, if you don't want to do what I asked?" Dad said in an unusually gentle fatherly voice. I was his only child with the courage to stand up to him.

He asked, "Would you take Mimi on your trip to Israel?" Mimi was Dad's sister-in-law, who was living with him and Fran. Without hesitation, I replied in a booming voice, "Noooooo!" and gave no explanation. I didn't say this to Dad, but Mimi was an alcoholic, sixteen years older than me, and hard to be around.

After my answer, Dad was speechless. Then I continued, "I have a mind. I know what I want to do, and don't have to do what you want me to do." This was our only great heart-to-heart father-daughter talk ever. I was nervous that Dad would then yell at me. Instead, he shocked me with his calmness and openness: "You know, Faith, I admire and respect you for standing up to me. You are just like me—stubborn, obstinate, and not afraid to stand up for your beliefs."

Our little talk, while I was a college student, drew me closer to Dad. He also revealed he was delighted that I was doing a "great job" with my life. I never knew that. Dad once told me I had his personality. He thought he was my role model.

By this time, Dad had created a mess—a blemished family turned inside out with divorce and a blind black sheep daughter wallowing in a well-off family. Dad was dominating and intimidating.

If Dad demanded you do something, God, you did it! We were all afraid of him. The three of us—me, Morley, and Shelly—didn't stand up to Dad. But I finally did, with what I learned from *Alice in Wonderland*. When the Queen of Hearts threatened to decapitate Alice, she stood up for herself. I learned to use my voice LOUDLY when I was being mistreated.

Sometimes it's tough to stand up for your ideas. But if you don't, it can hurt your mental well-being. I've since stood up for my beliefs. This improved my life tremendously. I stick to my guns. That builds my self-confidence, my identity (sense of self), self-respect, integrity, and self-sufficiency.

Dad always encouraged us children to make our own decisions. And I was prepared to do that. I decided that there was only one way to keep my sanity: Get away from the crisis and go to college out of state.

My closest friends were going to go to Roosevelt University or the University of Chicago downtown. They would continue living with their parents. But I wanted to go away from the divorce mess at home. I wanted to be responsible and accountable to myself for my actions and be challenged by a new adventure. I decided to major in education at Indiana University, 230 miles from home.

Going away to college was one of the most terrifying but thrilling times of my life. I was scared shitless. I had to suck it up—put on my big girl panties—and just go. It was like closing the door on a former life and starting a new one.

College was going to mold me into the person I wanted to be. I was excited and hopeful of this becoming the happiest four years of my life. I earned it after the disastrous catastrophes I faced at home.

Once there, I loved walking among its sweet-smelling magnolia trees and stately buildings, a welcome lifestyle change. Life at Indiana University was the same as high school—without Mom and Dad and fewer rules. One of my most significant transitions in life was going from high school to college. But it wasn't so bad. No one told me when to get up or go to bed, do my homework, or what to wear. I wasn't even required to go to classes. But I did.

PART 2 WAS DAD A BAD SEED?

I could drink all the alcohol I wanted in college. But I wasn't a big drinker. Dad introduced us kids to liquor at home as early as age thirteen. He had us taste a variety of liquors, so we knew their "effects when we dated." All of us socially drank a lot with Dad when we lived at home. He drank quite a few scotches.

In 1946, Morley and I celebrated his graduation from Dartmouth College at the Palmer House in downtown Chicago. He invited me to have a cocktail with him. I was so ashamed. I had never had a cocktail before. I was eighteen years old. I said, "I don't know what to order." Morley replied, "You seem to like Scotch," remembering our home tastings. I'll order you a Rob Roy. It's a Manhattan made with Scotch."

I wanted to be grown up. The Rob Roy was potent and tasted like medicine. I drank half of it and spilled the other half on the table. I don't know if it was an accident or if I did it on purpose. I was humiliated, but Morley rescued me, saying, "Smart, sister. Remember to do that on a date. It's better to waste the liquor than for you to get sick." I used his tip many years later to get out of a socially awkward situation on a singles group overnight trip.

At Indiana, my life improved like never before. It was a new, stimulating life that gave me time to myself to emotionally heal from troubles at home. Soon I was ready to take on the world myself. That was until I found out Dad was divorcing Mom. The world collapsed around me—again, and I didn't know what to do.

After we all knew of the pending divorce, Dad reminded us children, "… You must always love each other, stay close, and see each other often…"

At my dorm desk, I spent a lot of time dreaming about finishing college, starting my adult life, and having a productive career. I looked forward to the day I'd really be on my own.

I wanted a man in my life. I saw that all my friends had sweethearts. In my sophomore year, I met Paul, my first real serious relationship. I thought I was madly in love with him. Paul and I decided to marry after the end of my junior year.

In the middle of that year, I was planning our wedding. But I couldn't concentrate on my studies. I was overwhelmed with the responsibility of deciding the marriage details. I told Dad I wanted to drop out of college and come home to plan my wedding. He was disappointed in my decision, but he said he understood.

I left college, came home with my head held high, and on a mission to plan a fabulous wedding. I was a good-hearted kid and wanted to continue my education. I had big dreams for the future—teaching young children. Dropping out was as much a tragedy to me as students leaving school because of a family death or financial problems. I didn't think I was throwing away three years of a college education.

I was home, and it was getting close to the wedding date. My college roommate, Liz, called me. She disclosed, "I hate to tell you this, but I think you should know, Paul is dating Betty."

Aghast, I wailed, "What! You've got to be kidding!" I announced to my family, "That does it! The wedding is OFF! I'm canceling it." I know why Paul started seeing Betty. I told Paul, "You'll have to wait until we're married to have me sexually." He said he understood. I lost him. I was such a prude. But that's the way it was in college. If you wouldn't go to bed with someone, you got dumped.

Ironically, my fiancé cheating on me was eerily reminiscent of Dad cheating on Mom. When I told Dad I called off the wedding with Paul, he commented, "It's better now than later."

I didn't want a husband cheating on me. And I certainly didn't want Paul anymore. He was wishy-washy and didn't mean it when he looked me in the eye and said, "I love you." I returned all the wedding gifts. I took my trousseau back to the store and gave my bridal nightgown and robe to my friend Alice for her marriage. For a few months, I had puffy eyes and was acutely miserable. But I gradually got over it.

Dad saw me moping around and asked, "Do you want to go back to college in September?" Dad said he'd pay for the rest of my college. I said, "No. I've messed it up. It's my fault. I'm sorry, I'm not going back to Indiana!"

I told my father, "I'll finish my last year of college myself in Chicago. I did this to myself. But I don't want your money. I've loused it up, and I will pay for the rest of college myself. I'll get a job and work it out."

I didn't know how long that would take.

I didn't want Dad's college money any longer. I felt so bad for Dad. He lost a helluva lot of money on the nonrefundable deposit for the hotel reception. I refused to be a coattail-riding daughter leeching off Dad's wealth.

I told Shelly, "I won't ever ask Dad for a penny. I'm going to stand on my own two feet and won't be beholden to Dad. I want to prove to him that I can make it on my own." When I was in a money crunch in the past, my sister used to holler at me, "You're so dumb. Why don't you ask Dad to help you? Why are you doing this on your own?" I never asked Dad for cash or trips before this. He usually just gave me money without me asking—and then wanted to give me more, which I declined.

But no more.

I was just getting over Dad and Mom divorcing. And now this. I contemplated if I could ever trust a man again. I made a rash decision to marry Paul, quit college, and refuse Dad's money to go back to college. I was doing well in college, and then I threw it all away. I kept telling myself, "It's all my fault." "It's all my fault"—over and over again. I "loused up" my life over a man and kept punishing myself for it for 20 years. How could I get out of this by myself?

For ten years, I bounced around in a series of mostly crappy part-time jobs, helping people buy furniture, cars, and homes. At the same time, I attended a few classes at local colleges and a dance school. My first boss fired me for slow insurance contract writing. My eyes prevented me from doing a good job. I didn't blame the boss. It was my burden. I assumed my eyes could do the job. After that, I determined if my eyes could do a job properly.

Dad felt sorry for me for being fired and asked me to work in his home-building office in Chicago. I agreed and ran the switchboard, filed, and typed documents for a short time until Dad moved the office to the suburbs. I didn't have any contact with Fran. She was still his personal secretary with her own office.

At the office, Dad taught me to be spot-on, orderly, and acknowledge authority. First, he told me not to call him "Dad" in the office; I had to call him "Mr. Brickman." My first day, I said, "Daa . . . Mister Brickman." That was funny. It was hard to say "Mister Brickman" at first. I almost laughed out loud. Dad scowled at my mistake. He treated me distant at work to avoid charges of nepotism.

If I typed a two-page letter for him and made typos, I hid them with correction tape. But Dad quickly spotted them. He curtly ordered, "Retype this." He hated correction tape. I had to retype the whole letter, so it was error-free. I couldn't make any mistakes for Dad. If I did, he glared at me. My damaged eyesight repeatedly frustrated him. And he continually sent out negative vibes.

I didn't mind doing that extra work. I didn't get mad. I just told myself, "Wow, this is a good experience. I like things done right too." Dad's criticism of me was invaluable. I learned to type better and become more polished.

After I worked at Dad's office, I studied to be an interior decorator and designer. I worked briefly at a furniture store until it closed. The next jobs were at an auto dealership and a mortgage company, near a studio where I took ballet lessons.

I desperately wanted to return to college. I got into my college mess myself. I had to get out of it on my own. But it wasn't easy, monetarily and emotionally.

My world was shaken by my decisions. I needed some courage to move ahead. I had to look no further than my name, Faith. I thought of the expression, "Have faith! Everything will work out." That always gave me confidence, comfort, and encouragement that everything will be better tomorrow. It also reminds me of my faith in God. Trust in God gives me the strength to withstand any danger, difficulty, or worries in my life. That calmed me when I started worrying about Russia taking over the world at the start of the Cold War.

PART 2 WAS DAD A BAD SEED?

During my time off from college, I found my true identity. I developed stronger self-esteem by overcoming difficult—if not impossible—challenges for me. I stumbled with inferior eyesight in the business world. But then I got my mojo and self-confidence back.

By 1957, I had enough of the working world. I was serious about finally graduating from college. I went back to school. I enrolled at Northwestern University in Evanston. Then I switched to Roosevelt University in Chicago.

Ever since first grade, my dream job was to be a teacher. I taught my first class to my dolls at age six. Polly was in my class and three other child dolls about a foot high. Polly was my best friend from my pre-school days. I talked to her daily, and we would cuddle when we were sad. Polly comforted me through all my eye surgeries. Sometimes sis begged to attend the doll class. "Can I come, too," she asked. And I enrolled her. I addressed the class in a husky voice, "Today's lesson is we're going to read the book about Dick and Jane. Can you read the words with me? "See Dick run. Run Dick run."

I would quiz the dolls, sing with them, and give them little report cards. The four dolls were seated in small child-sized chairs at my little table with alphabet letters on it. I would fold paper, make little books the size of cocktail napkins for each of my "students," and put them on the table in front of each doll. By age ten, I didn't play much with dolls any longer. I instead spent most of my free time with a live "doll," Esther.

My teacher, Mrs. McKensie, inspired me to teach kids and follow the rules. She was the motivating element that drove my story (known as a MacGuffin). I badly needed to find my MacGuffin and hunted for it for a long time with little help.

At Roosevelt, I majored in education. It was a whole new culture than when I started college in the late 40s. Life moved quickly in what was called the Swingin' Sixties. My life was altered forever. I became a teacher, a wife, and a mother, all within a few years. Meanwhile, Americans witnessed the civil rights movement, President Kennedy's assassination, the Vietnam War, high prosperity, hippies, and beehive hairdos.

While student teaching, I discovered that I definitely wanted to be an educator. I graduated from Roosevelt in 1963 with a teaching degree. I didn't know it would take me sixteen years from quitting college, beating myself up, and finally becoming a teacher.

They say you often turn out to be very close to who you wanted to be when you were younger. I started chasing my dream to be a teacher at age six and actually became one at age thirty-six. I never gave up.

I can't believe I pursued my dream for thirty years . . . from giving Polly an "A" on her report card to stepping into a classroom as the teacher for the first time. Huzzah!

I could ultimately help change peoples' lives. I did it without my father's money. I did it the hard way. But I did it my way. I couldn't be any happier.

It was inevitable I would become a teacher—nineteen years after starting college. I learned from Dad that diligence pays off. He only achieved his goals through hard work. I saw how that taught him discipline, dedication, and determination. I realized this after watching him in his office.

Some people thought I'd never be able to teach children. They commented, "You can't be a teacher! You're legally blind." But I did anyway and did it well. Mom gave me the courage to go against the grain. I was assigned to teach special education pupils, and I used my creativity and vision handicap to help children learn.

The first day I said, "Class, move your seats close to me and the blackboard. I have an impairment, just like you. We're going to use the blackboard, and I will be able to see what you are doing." I taught them spelling, writing, and handwriting. I had kids create a sentence on the blackboard, underlining the spelling word. I told them to make it large enough so I could read it.

My first job was in the bustling Near North Side of downtown Chicago. At Ogden Elementary School, I taught mixed races, special education kids, ages six to fourteen, and two years behind their grade level. They were from rich and poverty-stricken white, Latino, and black families. Diagnosed as learning disabled, they were eager to learn, as I was excited to help them. They loved me, and I loved them.

Sometimes I would have my students in a circle holding hands—the black, tawny brown, and white blended together as they should. Someone asked me, "How many black and white children are in your class?" My answer was, "I never counted them that way."

After a year, I transferred to Linne Elementary School and again taught all special ed pupils. One of my pupils, Victor, asked me to come to his young mother's funeral. At the funeral home, I held his hand, and we tearfully walked together to say goodbye to his mother in her casket. Special ed at Victor's school closed at the end of the school year, and I would have to teach at another school in the fall. I loved watching my students grow and learn. They didn't want me to leave. I didn't want to go either. But I went with a sad heart.

I didn't know what was about to happen to me that fall.

Four unforgettable teachers stood by me and helped turn my life around. Mom gave me optimism. Dad showed me the advantages of hard work. Alice (in *Wonderland*) coached me on finding my identity. Ancient Greek storyteller Aesop taught me a lesson on perseverance. Dad also taught me exactness, family love and closeness, sticking to beliefs, and having a better day tomorrow.

I was in no rush to get a college degree, but I got there slow and steady. It was like one of Aesop's most famous fables, *The Tortoise and the Hare*. The slow, plodding tortoise (me) beat the overconfident, speedy hare (the world) in a race. The hare took a snooze during the race and woke up to see that the underdog tortoise had won. As a result of this story, my attitude that I messed up my life changed. I was no longer blinded by arrogance, and I used my perseverance to make up for my limited eyesight.

I wasn't the shamed black sheep in the family then. There was nothing, though, that humiliated our family more than Dad.

CHAPTER 11:
Murder, Greed, and Corruption

E verything was booming in the 1950s. The Korean War. The economy. And babies, including the births of my three half brothers, Robert, Michael, and William. It was the age of suburban paradises of identical pink homes filled with smiling housewives, pipe-smoking men, poodle-skirt-wearing girls, and freckled-faced boys. *I Love Lucy* premiered. Elvis earned his first No. 1 hit, *Heartbreak Hotel*. The space race took off.

After the war, Dad's business took off, too, like wildfire. He was a genius and prosperous. I admired him for helping many people buy affordable houses ordinarily out of their price range. He gave our family as much money as we wanted while generously donating to charities. But we had issues often found in wealthy, influential families: dark secrets, hidden skeletons, and intense sibling rivalries.

Dad's shady side emerged after he divorced Mom. His life makes me think about the 1975 Tony Award-winning musical, *Chicago*, set during the Roaring "Jazz Hot" Twenties. It's a scathing satire on making celebrities out of criminals whose crimes then seem appealing. Picture yourself in the theater, listening to the overture, watching the curtain go up, and being mesmerized by the opening number, *All That Jazz*:

ANNOUNCER: "Ladies and Gentlemen, You are about to see a story of murder, greed, corruption, violence, exploitation, adultery, and treachery. All the things we hold near and dear to our hearts." (Instrumental)

VELMA (singing): "Come on, Babe Why don't we paint the town? And All That Jazz . . . "

When I closed my eyes later and dreamed about my life story, I suddenly opened them. My right hand flew to my chest, and my fingers spread out in a fan against the breastbone. Oh, my gosh! I felt my racing heartbeat . . . I realized all the overture themes of the musical snaked their way through my deep, dark-secret Chicago life!

Murder. Greed. Corruption. Violence. Exploitation. Adultery. Treachery. All seven of them. All in my family for a century—from 1911 to 2015!

Dad was a prolific provider, but he turned out to be crooked. That was our family crisis. He disgraced our family more than I did. Trouble quickly grew. Dishonesty got the best of him at home, at work, and everywhere else. Dad treated me like the family's black sheep. And he committed adultery with his secretary.

CHAPTER 11 Murder, Greed, and Corruption

Vice was widespread in the Chicago construction industry, and Dad, as a home builder, was part of it. I met some of Dad's alleged mobster friends at a party at his house in the 1950s. They looked like they were in the underworld. Afterward, I checked their names with relatives. I was right! Dad got money from the Mafia, and it helped support our family. I believe Dad was a Jewish mobster, also known as the Kosher Nostra.

I'm not surprised that Dad may have associated with Capone and the Mafia. Dad, in his mid-twenties to the early thirties, and Mom were raising two toddlers (Morley and me) on the South Side. Our home was a couple neighborhoods away from Capone's residence. Capone dominated Chicago organized crime during Prohibition. Dad was a stickler, as was Capone. Dad shared many Mafioso qualities—100 percent sociopathic (only focused on his own personal needs), greedy, generous, fierce, self-centered, and ambitious.

Father's' home-building business was in Chicago and its suburbs, riddled with proven widespread bribery, graft, and extortion. Newspaper articles showed that Dad aggressively pushed government officials to change zoning regulations so he could build homes. Dad used lawsuits and intimidation to get what he wanted as mobsters do. Sometimes Dad paid off officials by donating money or buildings to cities, considered a bribe. It would not surprise me, though, if he bribed people with money. Everyone else was doing it.

Dad lacked integrity. He was corrupt in the most corrupt place in America—Chicagoland. Living in Chicago and its suburbs, I think he thought nothing of violating business or social ethics, committing crimes, and devastating Mother Nature. Dad had a big ego. He seemingly walked all over other people to get what he wanted without caring how his actions harmed them. Dad deceptively embellished advertising, stating he was a home builder longer than he really was.

Perhaps he was like this for the "love of family." He had enough money to buy almost anyone off if he wanted to. I felt sorry for Dad having to do some of those things to compete, survive, and put food on our dinner table. Dad was driven to be successful and provide for his family. I never saw him being greedy.

I witnessed Dad commit treason to his country and me. He violated laws, breaking his pledge to be a loyal citizen in the nationalization oath of allegiance that he took in 1930. He swore to "support . . . laws of the United States of America . . . without any . . . purpose of evasion."

He betrayed my confidence in him by lying when he promised me money in his will. He also cheated on and lied to Mom and in business. Uncompromising, ethical people, like me, think cheating and lying are the biggest betrayals in life. We want to do what's right.

CHAPTER 11 Murder, Greed, and Corruption

When I started writing this book, I discovered that Dad was a scoundrel in business who tarnished the Brickman family name. I tried to remember him by the positive things he taught me about life—money management, excellence, optimism, and verbal skills. This helped me let go of negativity in my life and become more positive and successful personally and professionally.

But I couldn't get over the murders of Dad's father and son, Bob. My father had nothing to do with them. But they saddened our whole family. Especially me. I lived forty years on the deadly streets of Chicago with the likes of Al Capone, John Dillinger, mob bosses, and street gangs. I never worried about my safety. I was more concerned about other family members.

I'm still distraught about the death of my half-brother Bob in 2015. My sister-in-law, Maria, accidentally or purposely shot and killed him.

My family was personally involved in the grisly shooting scene, which I call "Familicide: Til murder do us part." (WARNING: If you are squeamish about graphic murder scenes, do not read this section. This is my commentary based on my knowledge and a newspaper report of the trial.)

Fran wasn't the evilest woman in Dad's second family. It was my sister-in-law Maria. She shot and killed my half-brother Bob with a twelve-gauge shotgun blast to the left-back side of his head. It was a ghastly first-degree murder scene late one August night of 2015 at their secluded vacation cabin in the heart of the Appalachian Mountains of North Carolina.

The first sheriff's deputy who arrived at the scene said the house was quiet. He knocked on the door and announced himself, saying, "Sheriff's Department, can we come in?" Then Mrs. Brickman started screaming hysterically. He entered gun drawn, finding every light lit, and Bob lying on his back. Still breathing, Bob was in a large pool of blood, with more blood everywhere. "It was more blood than I have ever seen at a crime scene," testified the chief investigative detective.

In her pajamas and barefooted, Maria was splattered with blood head to toe. Deputies found her sitting on the floor, trying to push the left side of Bob's brain back into a five-by-three-inch wound in his head. His loaded .380 Ruger® handgun was found lying near him. It was covered by so much of his blood that detectives couldn't read the serial number. Shotgun pellets were lodged in kitchen cabinet doors near the front entrance. It was unclear whether Bob threatened her with the handgun or whether Maria planted his pistol after she shot him.

Bob, seventy, wearing wet shoes, just entered the cabin, and a heated argument started. Cuban-born Maria, fifty-six, hurriedly got the shotgun from a spare bedroom. Then she ejected an unused round (found in the fireplace) to make sure a live round was in the chamber, according to the assistant district attorney. She shot Bob while he was taking off his shoes. She told an investigator she thought the shotgun was loaded with practice rounds, inert dummy bullets that do not fire.

The prosecution speculated Maria could have been waiting in ambush for Bob to come home. Only she knows. Maria, his third wife, hysterically called 911, which captured her saying, "Why, why Bob? I love you." Bob died on the way to the hospital, leaving four sons from two previous marriages, brother Mike and three grandchildren. Bob was married three times, each lasting from eleven to eighteen years. It might have been her third marriage too.

A couple weeks before the shooting, Bob, a self-employed attorney, filed for bankruptcy. I think they previously fought, got divorced and then got back together a few years before the shooting. Married at least eleven years, the couple dabbled in business ventures from their home. Their $340,000 single-family, two-bedroom pool home was in the Belle Lago gated community in Fort Myers, Florida. For a change of pace and hunting, they went to their $162,000 wooded cabin beside a small creek in Murphy, North Carolina.

As to Maria's motive, the prosecutor claimed that she no longer loved Bob. She was angry he couldn't afford to give her beautiful things anymore.

PART 2 WAS DAD A BAD SEED?

Her defense attorney said she was not guilty of murder. She shot him in self-defense. Bob started taking his financial troubles out on his wife two years earlier, her attorney said. He almost beat her to death then, requiring emergency hospital treatment. It was like Maria was saying, "I didn't intend to kill him. It was an accident that he provoked."

In mid-2018, a jury in Cherokee County, North Carolina, quickly found Maria not guilty of murder after three and a half hours of deliberations. She's free. Thought she'd never get out of jail. The trial lasted one week. It was expected to go much longer in Murphy, the low-income populated county seat.

Seven women and five men originally sat on the jury. One male jurist quit during deliberations over "arguing . . . not getting nowhere" and saying, "I have to go to work." In his absence, the seven-women, four men jury came back to the judge with a unanimous not guilty verdict. The lead defense attorney said the verdict was as fast as he's ever seen in a murder case. I can't believe she was set free. It makes me vomit. She blew Bob's brains out. Our family thinks the trial was a farce, with improperly dressed hillbilly jurors who didn't know what the hell they were doing.

I think Bob's wife got off easy. It was an awful tragedy that I'm still shaking my head over it. I loved Bob. He looked a lot like Dad and had a pleasant smile. Such a nice guy. Bob had two younger brothers, Mike, and William, who died in 2004. I have five siblings and half-siblings, and two of them are alive—Shelly, eighty-six, and half-brother Mike, seventy-one.

Poor Dad. So much tragedy, cheating, and dysfunction in all his families—his family of origin, first family, and second family. Dad himself was a little . . . strange. What went wrong? Was he just a "bad seed?"

Dad had one last lesson to teach me about life . . .

[Page Intentionally Blank]

CHAPTER 12:
Rags to Riches to Rags

Dad's was the kind of classic, self-made success story that is revered in America. A poor Russian immigrant becomes a self-made millionaire by age forty-nine through hard work and strength of mind. He wanted more money, fame, and power. But something unexpected happened that turned his world upside down.

In this chapter and the next, Dad is the focus of my story because he influenced my whole life. Remember, experts say a father affects all a child's relationships from birth until death. Throughout life, girls look for qualities in men and other people based upon what they learned in childhood, particularly from a father.

Dad started his home-building company in the early 1940s. He had to prove himself against feisty American home-building competitors at the end of World War II. The housing market was booming. Developers could make a killing if they built in the right places at the right prices.

My father became fascinated in the late forties by another developer's plans for a new community, Park Forest. Park Forest rose on 3,000 acres of cornfields, south of Chicago. By 1954, it housed more than 3,000 families and was named an All-America City. Dad was inspired by that idea. He wanted to top it in the prime sheep-raising fields of Kildeer, where he lived. And he earnestly set out to do it.

In the late 1950s, Dad announced he wanted to build a "billion-dollar city" (eight billion dollars today) in the countryside of Kildeer. The town was a wealthy, secluded Chicago suburb in the northeast corner of the state. He planned to turn the village of 132 people into a busy city of up to 80,000 people, about the size of Evanston, Illinois. Dad boasted, "This will be the largest planned community in the United States."

Most Kildeer farmers and local residents didn't want Dad destroying thousands of acres of beautiful countryside. That's what attracted residents to live there—fertile, rolling, heavily forested land, with streams and small lakes. Many opponents thought Dad was greedy, aggressive, and deceitful. The Long Grove village president called the plans "grandiose," "presumptuous," and a surprise because residents weren't consulted beforehand.

Chapter 12 Rags to Riches to Rags

Others said his audacious plan was just a "get-rich-quick-scheme."

Yet, my father dug in for a bitter two-year battle, rich with illegal shenanigans. First, Dad started building on the proposed site without the required approval from the village. He put up quite a few three-bedroom homes and moved barns and sheds on to the land. Then Dad moved hundreds of migrant farmworkers, transients, and his nearby office employees and agents into the structures. Dad called for an election to incorporate the proposed site as a village, and he had the votes stacked in his favor.

He bribed his new residents: "You vote 'Yes' in the election," he told migrants, "and I'll give you free housing." He promised employees, "Vote 'Yes,' and I'll rent your unit to you for only fifty-dollars-a-month." Of course, Dad would control the new village and the people who ran it. He exploited and manipulated the farmworkers. Ruthlessly, Dad cheated, lied, and manipulated people throughout his career, I believe.

Leading up to any vote was a vicious battle of words, physical fights, and many legal suits. The controversial home-building proposal brought out the worst in people. Dad put his life on the line. Opponents shouted obscenities and fought with clenched fists.

One Saturday in 1959, the struggle got nasty between residents and Brickman workers, who were moving a barn to migrant-occupied land. The two sides stood off at a bridge, taking "on tones of land battles of the Wild West," reported the *Chicago Tribune*. It was a David versus Goliath clash—jostling, shoving, uncontrolled tempers and fights. As a warning, resident Rudy Huszagh pumped a rifle shot into the ground to stop a truck carrying the barn. Yet, the fighting continued until broken up by Sheriff's deputies.

Dad faced endless rezoning tussles and lost four legal battles, including one in the Illinois Supreme Court.

Finally, the proposed development failed. Kildeer residents voted to incorporate the entire village—not just Dad's proposed site—and restrict residential and commercial development. This legal step had never been done. Other nearby villages did the same thing, stopping materialistic developers. Kildeer residents celebrated and ran Dad out of town. He sold project property and his nearby estate, Long Grove Farms, where he strove to influence gentlemen farmers and newsmen at parties and rodeos. Dad did one good thing in Kildeer. He helped it grow more orderly. Kildeer leaders have since lured affluent homebuyers, maintained tranquility, and turned away greedy developers like Dad.

His life was never the same again. His rapid rise from rags to riches turned out to be a nightmare for him, our family, and me. The Kildeer pressure upon him was enormous. The emotionally stirring disaster got the best of father. It hurt his mental health and business. My father paid a hefty fee in Kildeer. I think his battle there killed him. Dad reportedly got sick, moved to upscale Lake Forest along Lake Michigan, and watched his hair turn white. And wait for the next disaster.

Dad's business had a storied history. By the early 1950s, the flagship company, Brickman Home Builders, was known as one of the biggest home-builders in the Chicago area. Dad's company became the dominant residential home builder in many Northwest Chicago suburbs. His sales of home, school, and apartment construction reached eleven million dollars in 1957 alone. Before 1968, he founded and built Highland Park Country Club and a twenty-one story Chicago apartment building.

Joe Brickman quickly became rich and was famous around Chicago. *Time* magazine hailed his success in a story and a picture of him.

Father was very innovative in the industry too. For instance, you could try living in a Brickman Manor townhome before you bought, with a rent-to-own agreement, believed one of the first such plans in America. He also pioneered in designing "perfect kitchens" that were conveniently arranged. They contained gas ranges that cooked with a heated cushion of air, not a direct flame. Newspaper photos showed Dad demonstrating to a young mother how she could fry an egg on a paper plate. But Dad's most critical challenges were just ahead.

PART 2 WAS DAD A BAD SEED?

Dad had the knack for having the right plan at the right time. By the mid-1930s, the Chicago area was way over subdivided into lots, ripe for plenty of development. But the Great Depression and World War II squashed most building. Dad sold lots during the war and built houses on them near the end of the battle, ahead of competitors. After the mid-1950s, Dad cashed in again as droves of Chicagoans left the city for the sprawling countryside. He pushed deluxe split-level, 3-bedroom homes with large family rooms for $20,900.

Shortly after the Kildeer loss, Dad's financial empire starting crumbling. Debts soared. Perhaps he counted on income from the Kildeer development to pump up his bottom line. He owned back federal income taxes and had to make a crucial decision to preserve his personal assets.

He decided to start fraudulently transferring more than $1.2 million to his second wife, Fran, and her three sons, according to the government. That was a lot of money then. It would be worth more than ten million dollars today with inflation. A few years later, he supposedly transferred more personal assets into corporations, such as the Highland Park Country Club, owned by second family members.

In 1977, the federal government convicted Dad of evading federal corporate income taxes—a felony. He owed more than one million dollars or a total of three million dollars with interest. That's equivalent to five million dollars today. After hiding money from Uncle Sam, Dad had only 3,000 dollars left in his personal estate and was bankrupt.

Dad was convicted of income tax evasion, just like his former South Side Chicago neighbor, Al Capone. Capone served eight years in prison for his crime. Dad served no jail time. Dad's death saved him from going to jail for up to five years. Two months after conviction, he died of a brain tumor, only three days after his seventy-sixth birthday.

Some 20 years after Dad's death, the feds were still trying to collect money it said Dad owed them. A federal judge denied a motion by Fran and her sons to dismiss the case, involving federal tax liens against property transferred by Dad to them, according to the case file. I don't know if they ever got any money. I imagine Dad's life of lust, greed, and crime—his deadly sins—was like a Hollywood movie. It was a rags-to-riches-to-rags story. It has adultery and womanizing, corruption and mob ties and the fate of becoming a convicted felon.

It's a shame, Dad didn't seem to enjoy his wealth while he had it. I pictured Dad living the lazy life of the idle rich, sipping a Scotch and water on a sunny Florida beach.

It didn't happen.

He slaved at work. He rarely took time off to enjoy himself, except a few times he vacationed in Florida with family. Once he caught an enormous sailfish in Bimini, and that brought a smile to his face. In the end, Dad lost everything he worked so hard for—his dignity, his first family, his money, and his life. Fran was just as deceitful as Dad. I feel she stole the first family's inheritance from Dad.

A widow, Fran continued to enjoy luxurious living for the next three decades with the help of Dad's money. She continued living in their off-Lake Michigan home in Lake Forest, among the nation's wealthiest cities. Fran also lived in several places in Florida with her sons. Right after Dad died, she got approval to build a resort condo in Treasure Island on Florida's beautiful Gulf Coast.

Dad chose the life he wanted to live. It might have been inevitable to him, but unexpected to me. I don't think anyone anticipated him to end his life practically broke and a convicted criminal. But he sacrificed his future for his second family. Dad discovered that money and power won't make you happy or successful. I thought it did when I was young. As I got older, I no longer believed that.

I learned, as David Pollay wrote, the more you think positively, the more likely you'll be successful and happy every day in life.

Dad had good intentions as a young man. But he turned into a monster as an adult, losing his morals through romantic flings and bad financial decisions.

He was like media mogul Charles Foster Kane of the film *Citizen Kane*. Kane's journey took him from an idealistic young man to a complete narcissist. Kane used his media empire to manipulate and deceived the public and the people around him. He died alone and lonely at the top. Dad and Kane: Characters driven to be the best there are in their occupations. Both abandoning or betraying people and everything they valued, such as honesty and closeness to family. For what? Fulfilling their magnificent obsessions, but winding up bitter, alone, and dying miserably.

Dad was drunk with power. He had his chance to make a meaningful mark in the construction industry. But I believe Dad's ego got entirely out of control, and he turned into a dictator. His biggest building project failed to get off the ground, and he fell into complete paranoia, thinking that residents and everyone else were plotting against him.

Even his first family . . .

PART 2 WAS DAD A BAD SEED?

[Page Intentionally Blank]

PART 3:
REBIRTH JUST IN TIME (1966-2020)

[Page Intentionally Blank]

CHAPTER 13:
Stolen Emotions

Father stole all my emotions with his strict rules. I couldn't love. I couldn't make decisions. I was indifferent. I couldn't trust people. I couldn't try new things and have gut feelings. I was stuck with low self-esteem and following peer pressure. Many of my friends had serious relationships, and I decided I wanted that too.

I just had no feelings at all. Dad fed me well but emotionally starved me. He neglected me and psychologically abused me. He passed on his troubled childhood problems to me, and they walloped me later in life.

This is what happens to kids growing up with an authoritarian father, according to experts. My emotionless dad stifled my feelings. If I showed emotions or swore, I'd get into trouble with Dad. He thought showing reactions was a character weakness and not manly. Dad himself rarely showed affectionate gestures in front of us.

Dad thought that strictness would make me stronger and behave better. But it actually made me behave worse and get punished more than other kids.

Once Morley and I burnt a pot making toffee candy, and we couldn't get it clean. Crossing her arms, Mom fumed, "That was my favorite pan. Wait till your father gets home." I never wanted to hear that. Mom punished us kids most of the time. But if we were awful, she'd call in the enforcer.

Dad was furious that we burnt a pot. He spoke sharply at us, "You shouldn't be doing that when you don't know what you're doing. No movies this Saturday for you both and Shelly." If one of us kids did something wrong, Dad would lose his temper, holler, and punish all three of us. Even little Shelly. No matter who was at fault! No movies. No ice cream. For everyone. Shelly would cry, "We can't go to the movies on Saturday . . . We can't get ice cream. Baaahaaaa."

My father never laid a hand on us, but something important would be taken away from ALL of us!

As a result of Dad's harshness, I couldn't tell if I was in love with a man or even recognize a casual or serious relationship with him. I was aloof with men, and that was one of the most significant crises in my life. I even found it hard to love George when he proposed to me. I just couldn't accept his genuine affection. I wasn't able to tell him, "I love you," until we got engaged at age thirty-nine. There was a reason I couldn't love until late in life.

At home, Dad did not reinforce the concepts of love and trust. I never understood love in my first few years of life, as most kids do. I learned from Mom that she cared for me and was on my side. But Dad didn't strengthen those basic ideas of relationships when he treated me with near hatred. I learned from Dad that if I followed his rules and minded him, I got his respect. If I didn't, I got punished and no love. I didn't have healthy relationships with people, caused by Dad's don't-trust-don't-feel rules.

I was almost forty years old, never married, and still living with my parents. I felt the social stigma of being an old maid who couldn't snag a husband. People talked behind my back about me. Men joked, "She's so chilly, you need a sweater to go near her." I desperately wanted and needed to love a man. But Dad denied me what I desired most. A woman then who couldn't catch a husband was considered a pathetic loser. I didn't think of myself that way at all. I was a new elementary school teacher who was gratified with my life.

After I started dating, I figured out why I was standoffish with guys.

I thought something was wrong with me, and I agonized over it. But it was really something wrong with Dad. I didn't realize that then. I dated a lot of guys from high school on. I could only think of them as good friends. We shared common interests, and we were not romantically or sexually involved.

I finally got a serious marriage proposal. I almost blew it by delaying my decision for more than six weeks. I believed I was at fault, not Dad. Time to beat me up again emotionally.

I started dating, then all of a sudden, I was competitively seeing Bob and George at the same time. I really didn't have any romantic feelings for either one of them. Bob was my torrid sex partner. George was my master bridge partner. With stakes increasing, the story got more intimate, personal, and nasty.

I thought I was in love with Bob, who taught me everything I needed to know about sex. But it wasn't genuine love. I just loved the sex. He was fantastic in bed. I swore I would never have sex with a man until I got married. Bob, broad-shouldered and tall with a charming smile, was very forceful. All my girlfriends were having sexual intercourse. I longed to be completely loved. I thought I'd marry Bob anyway. My heart controlled my mind, and I never regretted it.

I met George at a singles group in the mid-1960s, we became weekly bridge partners, and started dating. He was a nice Jewish boy. He was forty-two. Neither of us had been married, and we both lived with our parents. I wooed both Bob and George with cooking skills that Mom taught me. Then I fooled around with them with stuff Mom never taught me.

As soon as Mom went out to play cards, I'd have Bob over for an elegant, candle-lit, romantic steak dinner with a big salad and baked potato on good China plates. Another night, I'd repeat it with George. They both like the same food and devoured my fancy dinners.

George and I planned to spend the 1966 Memorial Day weekend together. But not overnight. I thought doing some browsing and eating together would give me something to do over the holiday. In the afternoon, we browsed antique stores and novelty shops on Devon Avenue. George bought me a beautiful bouquet of roses from a flower vendor.

Then he took me for a fancy dinner at DeLeo's. We sat at the bar, waiting for our table. George said, "I want to order your drink. It's special and hard to make. We'll watch the bartender make it. It's called a Pousee Café." That's a favorite nineteenth-century after-dinner drink made with several Technicolor liqueurs layered like a rainbow cookie.

We watched the bartender make the labor-intensive drinks for ten minutes. He filled special Pousse Café glasses with quarter shots of grenadine, dark crème de cacao, maraschino liqueur, orange curaçao, green crème de menthe and parfait amour, and a ½ shot of cognac. "Wow! I exclaimed. It's too pretty to drink." But George said, "Go ahead. Try it." I took a small sip, smacked my lips, and said, "It's GOOD—and strong." George chuckled.

At dinner, he ordered an exquisite meal for two: Chateaubriand and elegantly designed mashed potatoes. It was so good we licked our platters clean in a fancy restaurant. We sat there, enjoying our company together.

George ordered a special dessert that he said wasn't on the menu. Out of the blue, he said, "Faith, I've been waiting for just the right moment to ask you this. And I can't wait any longer . . . "I love you. Will you marry me?"

I thought something was up, but not a proposal. I felt like someone hit me from behind with a 2x4 board. To me, George was just a good friend. I was blind to clues that he was in love with me. Pun intended! I was breathless, and my heart was racing. I was not prepared for this. I was aloof, and I didn't know what to say. I took a playful swat at his hand. "I said, George, I thought we had a platonic relationship." Mortified, George bellowed: "Ah, ha-ha! You've got to be kidding me! HA-HA-HA!"

Despite his snark, I went on, "You know, I can't have children. To me, marriage includes a family. We would have to adopt a child." We were holding hands. He said without any hesitation, "I love you. Whatever you want, we will try to do." I wanted to have two children. But I had a hysterectomy at age thirty-four, and it's not possible to become pregnant and have a baby after that.

CHAPTER 13 Stolen Emotions

My heart wanted my other guy, Bob, the apple of my eyes. But my mind wasn't sure what to do. I was happy yet frustrated and bewildered. I didn't want to throw this wonderful man, George, away. But there's this other man, Bob, in the background.

Marriage was a big decision for me. I couldn't take it lightly. It would affect me for the rest of my life. I took a deep breath.

I held on to George's hand tightly and said softly, "George, I need to think about this. I'll give you my answer at Kal's party." His cousin Kal was going to have a dinner party for us on my birthday . . . forty-three days later! If we were going to marry, I thought that would be just the right time to announce it.

George was stunned and baffled. He must have been thinking: "Who is this lady? Why is she doing this to me? I know she can be hard to deal with, but this is ridiculous!" I thought to myself, "I'm absolutely stunned George didn't walk away from me right there." He gave me an incredulous stare or dazed look. George said adamantly, "I want you to be sure. Just remember, I love you. Whatever you want, including children, we will do."

I didn't know if George would stick around forty-three days for my answer. We went out the following week, and George was understandably upset:

— "I haven't been able to sleep all week. Why are you doing this to me? Look, if you aren't going to marry me, just cut me loose so I can go on with my life."

— *"George, I really think it's going to work out. But I need time to be sure."*

— "OK, You're making me feel a little bit better."

— *"You're right. You need to know my answer. And I will let you know. But not until the party."*

I was unsure of myself. I didn't want to screw up again with men as I did with Paul. I needed time to figure things out for myself. Silly me, I made it more complicated by continuing to date both George and Bob once or twice a week. George, my companionable friend, was trying to hold the edge. Bob was really playing me along. And I knew it. And I loved it. The sex was so good.

Even Mom and my girlfriend got on my back for my indecision. Mom: "Why can't you make up your mind already?" Girlfriend Barbara: "You should marry George. Bob's just using you for sex." I finally came to my senses and focused on the crucial points, not the sex. I wanted to adopt children since I couldn't have my own.

George really loved me and wanted to adopt. I'd be foolish not to marry him. He's got an excellent job, he's a hard worker, and he loves me. What more do I want?

I knew if I got married at age thirty-nine, I was not going to get divorced. I'd have a stable love triangle—my new teaching career, a husband, and a new child and family.

The day after George's proposal, Bob and I ate steaks at his favorite place, Miller's Steak House. He was close to asking me to marry him. I was madly in love with him—I thought.

I said, "Bob, if we were to marry, you know I can't have children. Marriage, to me, includes a family. We would have to adopt a child. Would you be willing to do that?" I thought he would answer saying something about his child from his failed marriage. Instead, he said, "I can't see raising someone else's child." Bob certainly didn't love me. He just used me for sex, like so many men use women as just play toys. But I used him for sex too!

Nobody knew whether I would pick George or Bob, not even me, until the last moment. Finally, I formally announced my answer at Kal's birthday party for me. I said, "George, I'm sorry I made you wait so long, but my response to your proposal is . . .

YES, I'll marry you!"

I got thunderous applause from the party guests. George and I passionately kissed and hugged. Wanting to waste no more time, we set the date to marry the next month. Let the dancing begin. I had a feeling that our platonic friendship would not continue as platonic life-partners.

But things changed overnight after I accepted his marriage proposal. We couldn't wait any longer. George and I shacked up together for the first time. It was a spontaneous moment . . .

After the party, I told Bob I was going to marry George: "We're done." Bob was my false soul mate, who seemed ideal for me at first but was a mismatch in the end. I burned Bob. Bob would not go away quietly. Even after I married George, Bob kept asking me out.

Imagine, I made George wait more than a month for my answer to his marriage proposal. It was hard to get out of the casual friendship that I had with him. I really made that man suffer. I didn't mean to. I just had to be sure I wanted to marry him than be sorry. I can't believe I did that. So horrible. I was a nasty girl then. I was naive about a man's feelings.

I regret the way I treated George when we were dating. I thought he was a casual friend, but that wasn't the case. I was oblivious to his love. He was in love with me and wanted to marry me. I had no idea. I'm lucky he really loved me and stuck around. I was afraid of divorce, because of my parents, if I didn't make the right decision.

George and I wanted to live together for a while and get married the next summer. You know, take it for a test drive. None of our friends had done this. Many young people do this today. I didn't know how to tell this to my conservative mother. Finally, I got up enough nerve and asked her about George's suggestion:

—I sheepishly said, "Mom, ah, George and I want to take our honeymoon now—live together—and get married next summer."

—"What?" Mom screeched with wide eyes, showing the whites. "You can't do that! You have to be married first."

Sex was once considered more sacred and special than it is today. Before the 1960s, some people, like me, refused to have premarital sex—period. Others did not have physical relations unless they were in love or were ("the rule") married.

Then came the sexual revolution in America in the 1960s, which influenced me. Some flag-burning liberals said it was OK to have sex just for fun. The shift in morals was caused by the introduction of the birth control pill. As a result, women became freer with sex. The pill worked better than condoms.

Now women were more assured of not being saddled with a child out of wedlock, frowned upon more than today.

In 1966, I had my first sexual relationship with Bob. I loved him and thought a love-sex affair was more permissible than before. We kept it hidden. We weren't as open with what we were doing as kids are today. If my mother knew, she would have "killed" me. I don't know about

Dad. He was promiscuous himself. He never questioned what I did with my life. But I don't think he would have been surprised if he knew I was having sex. I loved exploring life, doing, and seeing new things. Before my marriage commitment to George, I only slept with Bob.

More than five million women were on the pill then. Premarital sex was now more accepted. Moralists, though, were troubled by the belief that love excused premarital sex. I thought if you loved someone, it was OK to have sex, now an outdated idea. Love is no longer required for sexual intimacy.

Dad also made me indifferent about life. I didn't trust people. I didn't rely on them. I didn't have confidence in them, even those closest to me, such as my husband. I took essential people for granted—my husband and friends. I once was indifferent, apathetic, and disinterested in things happening in my life. They were just there.

I never thought about them much until I started writing this book. I don't regularly look back on my life. As I got older, I learned to appreciate what I still had, such as my husband (or memories of him) and friends. I now tell friends how much I enjoy them.

I also was frightened of failure, like Mom and Dad's divorce. I wanted to be sure I was going to marry the right man and make the right decisions. My daddy issue led to repeated dysfunctional choices in my relationships with men, such as falling for sex-seeking Paul and being indifferent to George.

Thankfully in marriage, comical interactions took my mind away from Dad stealing my emotions. At age thirty-six, I took a summer trip to Europe with Roosevelt University friends. I couldn't get a Rotterdam cruise ship reservation to come home on a specific date.

George, back in Chicago, got the booking for me. I got home and waited a week for George to call me. I was taught that the guy was supposed to call the girl. He finally called.

— "You're home?" acting surprised when he knew I was home because he arranged the trip.

— *"Yes, I've been hoping you'd call."*

—"How can I call when I don't know you're home?"

That's the type of comical type of interaction I enjoyed with George. He arranged this trip, and I should have realized he was serious about me.

Just before my marriage, I discovered how badly Dad damaged my natural emotions, including my ability to love. I made some excellent relationship decisions that changed my life in marriage.

I would never put my kids through what Dad did to us. I learned from Dad never to suppress emotions with my daughter and my grandchildren.

As a parent, I transformed into someone more insightful. I went from a feeble authoritarian-dominated child into a close-connected, nurturing, authoritative mom. I practiced open communication and understanding with

Naomi and her children. I gave them more self-dependence and freedom as they grew up than I had.

I felt guilty and ashamed of myself with emotional defects for not living up to my potential as a solid citizen sooner. But after I married and adopted Naomi, I decided to take control of my life. I thrived like never before—after my rebirth.

CHAPTER 14:
Redemption and Rebirth

L ife was beautiful. I was finally married to a good man, my bridge partner turned marriage partner. I had the love of my life and a dream teaching job, molding young minds. I was over troubles with Dad.

I had to pinch myself and ask, "Is this really happening?" I couldn't stop telling George how lucky I was to find him. At almost forty, I felt fortunate that I got a real happily-ever-after marriage and life.

George was handsome, five feet, nine inches, and had thinning dark brown hair. Under dark brown framed glasses, his penetrating, baby blue eyes followed me everywhere. He couldn't keep his firm, gentle manicured hands off me. His Old Spice cologne, with a mild manly aroma of sage and cinnamon, quickened my pulse. I picked a man who was like Dad. Both were firm. George was always neat and clean, like Dad and me. Unlike Dad, George was a caring father. He never had a cavity in his life. I had to laugh—I'm legally blind, and he was color blind.

My secret of a happy marriage: wait until after age thirty-five, when you have more wisdom and emotional maturity. New worldwide research confirms that waiting makes sense. Many women feel pressure to settle down in their twenties. And if they pass thirty, whoa . . . time to marry is quickly running out.

Entering marriage, I fell under the shadow of a dark power. It was my childhood shortcomings emerging— controlling domination and endless intractability. At first, things seemed to go well. As my sweetheart and I settled into married life, the dark power receded. Then on a routine shopping trip, it broke out with a vengeance. I needed to fix this predicament.

I was a good person. But the crisis was within me. I had bad weaknesses. I was very stubborn and damn spunky. Actually, I was too strongminded, manipulating, and self-sufficient for my own good. My out-of-step-with-life personality got me into trouble throughout my existence. George was also very determined. With two forty-ish, obstinate momma's kids, our relationship was already in trouble. Would we be continually arguing? Argh . . . Maybe we were incompatible? Rats, I couldn't believe that was true. I held hope everything would be OK. We both promised to work together, communicate, and understand each other.

CHAPTER 14 Redemption and Rebirth

The BIG question was whether I could resolve my conflicts with others, find joy every day, and lead a happy, productive life.

The primary threat to our marriage—my regulatory pitfalls—returned at full strength. My dark powers cornered me in a "living death" early in marriage. I was running virtually both my life and my husband's, everything from finances, travel, and even sometimes sex. It was a life destined for misery and void of joy and satisfaction.

I wasn't aware of how dominating I was. But George was.

A wife usually believes her new husband, but I didn't. I couldn't give myself to somebody else so completely. That's why I wanted to control our lives myself from the start. George, though, wanted to stifle my control obsession. Something had to give.

We needlessly argued over who would control the finances. I was a strong woman used to getting my way. I started entering in the checkbook and paying the bills, but George said, "That's the man's job!" The issue came to a head right after we got married.

George saw me buying a dress.

— George: "Let me pay for it."

— Me: "I'm working. And I've got the money to pay for it. I'll pay for it from my money."

— George: "I don't care! You're married. Your husband is supposed to do this. I want to pay for it. You're too damn independent!"

— Me: "George, if I can make it easier and quicker, this is ridiculous that you pay."

— George: "Why are you so stubborn? Why don't you let me manage the finances and pay for things you want to buy?"

I wouldn't let him pay for the dress. I fought and won. There's only one way, and that's my way. George was right. But I had trouble letting go of my financial freedom. These little battles continued for all of our forty-three years of marriage.

Also, we had little tiffs over roses. What girl doesn't love getting gifts of flowers and jewelry from romantic partners. When a man does something wrong, he'll probably give her flowers, particularly roses. If he really messes up, he'll give her jewelry instead of flowers. From the day we were married, George obsessively showered me with expensive gifts—roses, jewelry, and paintings. And he hadn't done anything wrong.

The gifts strengthened our bond, reinforced his feelings for me, and made him feel caring. George had discovered the greatest secret of happiness. His gifts to me gave him genuine pleasure and satisfaction. I have never been so loved in my entire life. George gave me too many gifts. He was a compulsive over-giver. Perhaps he was afraid of disappointing me. Maybe he thought I would see his love as real, rather than as a pre-marriage casual friend.

Giving gifts has always been an essential part of building healthy, love relationships. George overdid it. I'm sure he was a codependent gift giver. That heightened our control battle and my need for rebirth and redemption. George was a codependent trying to control me. He thought he was just generous. But his gifts came with emotional ties. He wanted to be admired and shape me.

What one thing could you give someone that's so beautiful and ups your sex appeal 1,000 percent? There's something about a rose, the traditional symbol for love and romance for centuries.

George was in love with roses, and I loved them too. He raised them in our backyard. Red roses are such an effective way to say, "I love you." They smell citrusy, fruity, and spicy, something like pumpkin pie. Their evocative, sweet aroma calmed me and improved my mood. George, beaming, looked really cool giving me any kind of roses. He devoured me with his eyes and melted me with his touch. Roses made us want to jump in the sack—and we frequently did!

For at least the first three years of marriage, I'd find a dozen red roses on the dining room table every Friday. I'd eagerly wait for that day all week. I wanted to be astonished. I entered the dining room, covering my face with my hands, and then peeking. Acting stunned, I'd smile, throw my arms around George and squeeze him in a tight bear hug.

But then one Friday, I showed George a tentative smile that built as surprise sank in. I found no newlywed red roses on the table. I said, "You know, George, I miss your roses." He said, "Well, you'll get them from now on for anniversaries and special occasions." I guess ordering a dozen red roses for 156 Fridays in a row can get tiresome and maybe meaningless.

At work on Wednesday morning, August 21, 1991, someone brought me a large bunch of red roses that had just been delivered. Curious employees gathered around me to see who they were from. I opened the card . . . They were from my heart-throb, George, for our twenty-fifth wedding anniversary. I was unexpectedly struck with a feeling of wonder. I was breathless. All I could do was smile and admire the flowers. George wanted to surprise me and say how much he still loved me. And he did that with thirty-eight textbook red roses. Don't know why it was thirty-eight.

"Oh, they're fantastic," exclaimed a coworker. Other employees laughed at the surprised expression on my face. "You're so lucky to have him," another woman said. "I know. I know," was all I could say, glancing about my coworkers for an escape. I couldn't rid myself of the attention, though.

CHAPTER 14 Redemption and Rebirth

The next day, Thursday, another thirty-seven red roses from George arrived at the office—a total of seventy-five roses over two straight days. I attracted even a bigger office crowd this time. And even more of the same type comments. It was just "Wow." Overwhelming. Obviously, I didn't get much work done that day—neither did much of the staff. They were all talking about my loving, sweet George.

I think he made it clear how much he loved me in front of everyone in my office. All my coworkers got roses to take home. After that, my colleagues often asked me, "Getting any flowers from George today?" I was the talk of the office for a very, very long time. George was extraordinary. George fell all over me. But he felt he wasn't showing me enough love. Eventually, I had to tell him, "Enough is enough, George!"

George was very talented. Besides raising Naomi while I worked, he was good with his hands. He made earrings, cabinets, fixed toys, and gardened. George was known for his rock collection (not music, but actual rocks) and moves on the dance floor.

He loved to give me jewelry on special occasions—anniversaries, medical milestones, trips, and more. On a trip to Alaska, he surprised me with a rare tanzanite blue, purple ring, mined at the foot of Mount Kilimanjaro in Northern Tanzania, eastern Africa. In Thailand, he bought me a lavender jade gold ring. When we adopted our daughter, he presented me with 18-karat gold opal tear-drop earrings and a bracelet.

Our married life also revolved around the basic comedy story plot. It isn't necessarily funny; it ends with everyone being happy, though. George and I were separated, then brought together. George and I were always destined to be together. He knew it, but I didn't. A series of light-hearted conflicts kept George and me at a distance. There was confusion, miscommunication, and frustration. George and I weren't entirely in sync.

But the confusion got even more complicated and escalated after I agreed to marry him. Turmoil followed over wedding details. Chaos is an excellent source of humor. The darkness separating us and the tension between us had reached their peaks.

Before marriage, Dad and I argued over where to seat some guests at the reception. I made the seating arrangements. But Dad moved some of my friends to sit with people they didn't know. It didn't make sense. Dad was just showing off his power. Our wedding was the first at the new Highland Park (Illinois) Country Club, north of Chicago. Dad built the club with his brother Lou and brother-in-law Rube.

George and I got our marriage license and completed all the other marriage paperwork. I was telling Ettie on the phone how excited we were. An operator cut into the conversation, saying George Block urgently needed to talk to me. I said to Ettie, "We've been arguing about marriage plans. I bet he wants to cancel the wedding." George told me there was a problem with the marriage license. He said, "The license is for Cook County, not Lake County, where we're going to be married."

Rabbi Burton, George's cousin, who was marrying us, proposed the solution: "I'll legally marry you in my study (in Cook County) after sundown Saturday night. Two people will witness my signature. On Sunday (the next day), we will sign the ketubah (the Jewish marriage contract). Then we will have the wedding ceremony in Lake County in front of all the guests." When the rabbi told us this solution, I gasped, saying to George, "Oh, George, what a story we have for our children." So we were already legally married before the big wedding ceremony. But few people knew.

That's not all.

We got through a few awkward ceremony moments. George's very English mother asked me to wear low heels at the wedding so George would be taller than me walking down the aisle. I didn't like his mother, defied her, and wore high heels. George was still slightly taller. As I passed Mrs. Block, she gave me a nasty glare. She was not warm or loving. When she later first saw our infant Naomi, she oddly remarked, "What a magnificent specimen."

Our dog-days-of-summer wedding on a rainy, mid-eighty-degree August 21, 1966, was one of the most glorious events in my life. About 150 people attended our wedding reception. Dad made sure it was first-rate, including a dinner of filet mignon and expensive Cadbury purple flowers table centerpieces. I felt like a celebrity. Camera flashes were blinding me. The pictures were to promote future club weddings. Shelly was my maid of honor. I think Dad was more nervous than I was. He was a half-hour late for the ceremony and forgot to wear his yarmulke.

Amid Vietnam War protests, our honeymoon night in Montreal was hilarious. It was a light comedy of errors that occurred before we arrived at Room 1002 in an expensive downtown hotel.

We had a late afternoon flight to Montreal for our honeymoon. It started to storm, and the rain was coming down hard, a good luck sign on a wedding day, according to superstition. Our best man, Herb, was responsible for making sure we left the celebration in time to catch our plane. He pulled us off the dance floor. We changed clothes, got in the car, and Herb dropped us off at the curb at O'Hare airport and left.

At the ticket counter check-in, we found out the plane was delayed by bad weather. Herb hadn't check to see if the flight was leaving on time. The trip was delayed for four hours. We could have had something light to eat and a romp in bed instead of sitting and milling around the airport until the plane left. George said, "Too bad Herb didn't check the plane's status. We were enjoying dancing, and here we are just sitting at the airport."

We got to the hotel around one o'clock in the morning and headed straight to our tenth-floor room. Both of us were hungry, tired, and longing to be in bed. George didn't even try to carry me over the threshold. We dropped our luggage and laughed loudly from tension and the delayed arrival. It lasted so long we thought the neighbors would complain about our behavior. We didn't stop laughing until we were breathless.

At last, we got into bed. George gently wrapped me in his arms and started kissing me all over. The rest came naturally and passionately for both of us. We had marriage intercourse for the first time. That was a fitting way to end our honeymoon comedy.

It was the beginning of a tender, loving relationship that spanned more than four decades.

I felt a great feeling of relief and happiness. I was married, and I would be with George every night. I'm glad I chose him. This marriage is what I wanted. Now it was really starting.

Unexpectedly, we immediately faced character conflicts. George and I were both independent and strong-willed. Strong-willed is different than being independent. Strong-willed people are very determined to do something, even if people think it shouldn't be done.

I brought unique qualities to our marriage. I was born strong-willed, committed to succeed on my own without any help. I exceeded my doctors' sight expectations. I became a motivational leader teaching children and counseling seniors. I fought more for my financial interests, such as being more demanding in salary negotiations and agitating my stepmom over not getting an inheritance from Dad.

I also had a disability superpower. Since I'm legally blind, I "see" with my ears and mind. I use my ears and memory to remember things, not my limited sight. Blind people have better memories than those with full sight. The blind use their memory to remember things. People say my mind is fantastic, and I can remember exact conversations much better than people thirty or forty years younger than I am.

I was known for my memory at work. Colleagues relied on my mind. Someone asked, "Faith, do you remember that client with the black hair? I can't think of her name. I think it started with the letter K." "Oh, yeah," I would reply. "That was Kathy Smith" or whatever her name was.

At home, George rescued me and redeemed me before it was too late. From an argument over a dress, he showed me my defects before they destroyed our marriage. My controlling-nature, mulishness, and self-support could have developed into arrogance, divorce, or being an old maid forever. George gave me the push I needed to see exactly how I was hurting our relationship and the world around me. I was used to doing things my way before my marriage. Now, though, I needed to change, grow, and learn from new experiences with George. I was reborn, a spiritual awakening that would start a new beginning with my husband.

George took away some of my independence and the need to resist change. I discovered how to tame my strong will by giving him more husbandry responsibilities. This was a life-changing decision I made that was inevitable and unexpected. I felt relief like I was reborn. This helped me focus more on teaching children.

Besides, George gave me emotional and physical stability in my life. We lived in only two homes in Chicago and Evanston. I previously lived my first forty years in more than a dozen different homes in Chicago and Canada, each only for a few years. Studies have found that kids who moved frequently are more prone to mental disorders, drug abuse, criminality, and unnatural mortality. I think my firm-will prevent the harmful effects of moving from penetrating my life.

George helped me, but I reluctantly redeemed myself. I relinquished some control for once in my life. I told him, "OK, George, you can run our finances and once in a while pay for a dress I want. I'll control our social and travel activities instead." George leaned back in his chair, more at ease and in control.

Giving up lifelong control was hard for me to do, but I had to do it. I finally learned to trust George. I could not have done it without his support and love. My rebirth gave me a spiritual regeneration, much needed for shattering events ahead.

CHAPTER 15:
Naomi, George, and Me

Right after I married, the nation and our lives were in a state of flux. But we couldn't be living better. The year 1968 brought the birth of our daughter and events "that shattered America."

Festering movements "exploded with force"—the aftershocks of the Vietnam War, the Cold War, civil rights, human rights, and the youth culture (Hippies). We ventured into the computer age, with the original computer the size of a house. We ate healthier—chicken and turkey. Broadcast television attracted huge audiences.

The first four years of marriage were riddled with mistakes, threatening our bonds and dreams. I needed to solve the catastrophe.

I was candid and honest in telling George that our marriage was off to a rocky start. My first mistake in marriage was moving into George's crowded, three-flights-up, one-bedroom apartment on the North Side of Chicago. Trains ran right by our windows, keeping me up at night. There was no air conditioning, making me uncomfortable and lazy. I wanted us to find a better apartment. But George, immovable as a mule, wouldn't move out. He said, "I'm not ready to move."

Meanwhile, we adopted a two-days-old baby girl. We worshiped our sweet content baby, a six-and-a-half-pound bundle of joy. George named her Naomi Elizabeth. Naomi means "God's promise," and Elizabeth represents "proud and pleasant." She was born, as Naomi says, "while we played bridge."

Naomi restored our faith in life and lessened our apartment and Vietnam War worries. She represented a joyful new beginning in life for our family.

When Naomi was nine months old, George and I moved our bed into the living room. It was challenging to host bridge games or have friends over. Our active, curious child got her own bedroom. We were going to look for a two-bedroom apartment.

But George lost his job before we could look.

George's boss told me at the company's 1968 Christmas party, "George is so productive and creative. He's going to go far in the company." George was head of the commercial department at Hallicrafter Corporation, a Chicago radio manufacturer. Four months later, George came home one day from work and sat beside me on our living room bed. Then he set off a bombshell. George said, "Faith, I don't know how to say this, but I was told today that my department is closing, and, at the end of the month, I will no longer have a job!" The company faced financial problems and was soon sold.

George completely broke down. He didn't believe in himself any longer. He regretted following his mother's advice not to become an engineer. I gave him optimism: "George, you can find another job, still be productive and support us and live a good life." But that didn't work. I don't know whether he even heard me. He was deeply depressed. He had no ambition to look for a job. My positive optimism became a negative trait. I made things worse, telling him to cheer up when my support had no chance of working.

We got marriage counseling. But I was miserable and took drastic action. Nine-month-old Naomi and I left George for two months. This was the shock he needed to try to find work in a weak job market. He took a few courses, got an education degree, and found a job teaching fourth grade in an inner-city Chicago school. We got back together then.

Naomi's presence alone gave George the incentive to find a new job. She encouraged repair of our broken relationship and strengthened our marriage forever. The magic of Naomi helped make everything better for us— and for her.

George got back on his feet, and we finally got out of the rat-hole apartment. In 1970, we moved to the town-home Dad gave us in upscale Evanston, just north of Chicago along Lake Michigan. This tree-lined Victorian city was ranked as one of the best places to live in the country. Hollywood filmmakers portrayed this college town as "the beau ideal of postwar suburban life."

Finally, something exciting was happening in our lives. In our new home, George and I decided to adopt a second child. The number of adoptions peaked at that time. Naomi was six. George set it all up with a lawyer, recommended by cousin Mimsi. George told me, "We can make the fee. So I'm going to go through with it."

We were both excited, except . . . When the baby boy was born, the lawyer called and doubled the agreed-upon price! The price may have jumped from something like $4,000 to $8,000. George never told me the amount, but he was furious. George said to the greedy lawyer, "No way, we're not paying you double the amount" and hung up. When we adopted Naomi, we paid only the doctor's fee for her birth, with no extra charges.

I pleaded with George desperately, "George, call the attorney back and tell him we'll pay him whatever he wants!" At forty-three, I was desperate to have a second adopted child. This was my last chance. I'd do anything. George said firmly: "No, I don't think it's legal. It could be a black-market baby that we may have to give up later." I knew by the unyielding tone of his voice, I could not argue with George. I rarely heard that harsh voice in our marriage.

People told us they had to return children adopted under suspicious circumstances like ours. State law said an adopted child had to live with adoptive parents for six months before a judge could finalize the adoption. We couldn't bear to go through something like that. And we were just not the kind of people who'd do something shady. Mothers then were selling their own babies or babies from Europe for the highest prices they could get. We were unnecessarily worried that Naomi's adoption might not go through too.

I wasn't mad at George for saying, "No." He acted in our best interests. I was angry with the lawyer, that rat. I knew in my heart that George was right. I was wrong. I regretted that we never got a second child. After our disagreement, I wept for three days. But then we found out that "our baby" was given to someone else, and the baby was not healthy. God was on our side.

After that harrowing adoption experience, I told George, "Let's not look anymore. The ages of the two children would be more than six years apart. I don't think that's good." There was a six-year age gap in my family between my birth and Shelly's. We were like two separate children—with different interests and friends. I didn't want that again.

PART 3 REBIRTH JUST IN TIME

Now, approaching my mid-forties, I was also afraid I would no longer have the energy to run around after a toddler. Did I really want even more sleepless nights? But I found out that family experts say there is no best age gap. Children closer in age can play well together. They are at the same developmental stage and share similar interests. Children with more significant age gaps may lose some closeness as the older child becomes a teen. There are pros and cons to everything. Most people adapt to age-gap situations without harmful effects.

I was such a dope. I felt I messed up again in my love life with this failed second adoption. The first time was dropping out of college and canceling a planned marriage.

If I recognized how serious George was about me, we could have married sooner, giving us more time to adopt a second child. This was the biggest mistake of my life. The clock just ran out on us. I know my authoritarian Dad psychologically created a barrier that prevented me from falling in love with George sooner. Yet, I just couldn't stop blaming myself for not adopting a second child. The emotional pain was noticeable physically. I saw unhealthy coloring on my face and dark circles under my eyes. I was hoping Naomi would get me out of my doldrums.

Some kids get away with most everything. They're spoiled brats. If they whine or scream, they get what they want. That wasn't Naomi. She wanted many things, and we were happy to give them to her. She was actually a "spoiled sweet." This is someone who gets her way, but as she grows up, takes "No" for an answer if her way hurts others. Maybe I'm a doting parent who gushes over how smart and talented she is, but she is. It's a fact. After all, Naomi was our only child. George and I made sure she had the best opportunities in life.

Naomi often got what she wanted, especially on special occasions. I wanted Naomi's special events to really be memorable. We were planning Naomi's Bat Mitzvah, a Jewish coming-of-age ritual, and party. She would be thirteen years old. She had gone to religious school since first grade and was having her Bat Mitzvah at the synagogue. We wanted the party at home.

Our Evanston townhouse was too small to hold more than fifty people for her party. So George and I bought a bigger house in Evanston just so Naomi would have room for her party! It was a two-story Cape Cod-style house, with two tall entry pine trees and a huge family room, at 815 Grey Street in Evanston. Just right for the party, although we were still fixing it up.

Naomi, on a trip to Hawaii, asked us, "Instead of me having a sweet sixteen party at home, can we come back here, please?" And we did. She wanted an expensive fiftieth birthday celebration in Las Vegas, and she got that too.

Naomi got athletic and artistic opportunities. She was a very active, strong-minded, and talented child. She sang and danced (ballet). She was offered a college violin scholarships and a job at a professional ice-skating company. We gave her swimming lessons before she was five and formal skating lessons at six. She loved anything with water, from playing with soap bubbles to swimming, to solo ice skating performances.

George tried to keep up with Naomi. Nothing stopped him, except himself. He was like my father, being obstinate and determined, but much more loving. George didn't know how to ice skate. But he insisted on skating with Naomi, a professional-level skater. She pleaded with him not to, fearing he'd make a fool of himself. Still, George bought expensive skates, strained to spin on the ice like his daughter, and fell. He was rushed to the hospital with a concussion. Good with kids, George spent hours playing and teaching our daughter and grandchildren.

My daughter was a handful. I needed to stop teaching for a decade to raise her. I loved motherhood. I belong to the Silent Generation, characterized by working hard and being family-oriented. George was an affectionate, strict father, but nothing like Dad.

Naomi impressed us with her way with words and her athletic ability. She was three when Grandpa Leslie died. We were in his apartment days later. Naomi went to his bathroom. She came out and said, "Grandpa forgot to take his toothbrush!"

At five, Naomi's tonsils were removed. We thoroughly prepared her for the experience. We gave her the book *A*

Trip to the Hospital and told her she could have all the ice cream and Popsicles she wanted after surgery. At home, I asked Naomi, "What would you like, ice cream or a Popsicle?" She whispered, "Mashed potatoes." I smiled. That was her favorite food.

My daughter is close to me today and appreciative of her upbringing. Naomi recently found her genetic parents and didn't like them. Naomi told me, "You and George are my real family, blood be damned." She was going to be adopted by another family instead of us. But we got her. We were a better match. At age forty-one, Naomi happened to meet her intended adoptive mother in a store parking lot. Afterward, on the way to the car with me, Naomi held my hand, looked me in the eyes, and said, "I'm glad you're my mother. You're the best thing that ever happened to me."

I raised Naomi for ten years and went back to work. I became the adult day care program coordinator at the Council for Jewish Elderly (CJE) in Evanston. CJE provides senior care and assistance services. I retired in 2005 at age seventy-eight and was honored for "25 years of dedication, expertise, and guidance."

I made the last years of peoples' lives fuller. I talked to hundreds of seniors. I'd ask, "Tell me what's bothering you? How do you feel today? What's going on at home?" Simple stuff. I sparked conversation and had time to give them. Their outlook often improved, helping them stay active for longer. My greatest joy was seeing happiness in them.

George retired from teaching in the mid-1980s after 20 years. He was a superior teacher. But that fall, he got stuck teaching a fourth-grade class with three disruptive, undisciplined, nine-year-old boys who didn't listen to him. He couldn't teach them, causing him emotional distress. The principal didn't split them up, so George retired. The teacher that replaced George quit after one month. He couldn't handle the kids, either. The principal then placed the rowdy students in different classes and asked George to come back to teach his old class. George refused.

He found lots of satisfaction elsewhere. George enjoyed a relaxed, part-time hospital volunteer job. My husband was a socializer but had a somber, intellectual side too. Often, he'd quietly do crossword puzzles. He had his mother's Manchester English humor. He could crack a joke without a smile.

He always gave me love, care, and understanding that couldn't be denied. He got all of my love in return. George was a hot lover. He loved holding hands and touching me when we were alone.

We enjoyed the greatest joys of life: romantic love and sexual attraction that never decreased in our long marriage. We still had sexual relations into our eighties until George got sick. Our sex drives were as strong as ever.

CHAPTER 15 Naomi, George, and Me

With regular sex, we felt happier in life than seniors who lost romantic interest.

I looked forward to the end of each day in bed with George. He always looked sexy to me. His words and gestures enticed and aroused my desire for him. I kept him interested in me by wearing new, lacy and sexy nightgowns, including short ones for "special occasions." I loved the feel of his body next to me.

We cuddled, kissed, and often fully enveloped each other. We never fell asleep without a hug and an "I-love-you" kiss. We kissed and cuddled more in the morning before we got up. Scientists have found that cuddling tends to make you happier, healthier, less stressed, sleep better, keep the heart healthy, relieve pain, and fight colds.

We never lost the joy of touching each other. Many times after George got home from work in the afternoon, we had sex. With so much cuddling, kissing, and sex, no wonder we lived so long. Mom advised me, "Never go to sleep angry with each other. Resolve your differences. Kiss and say, 'Goodnight.'" We never stayed mad at each other. Since his death, I haven't stopped thinking about him, especially in bed. It's so lonely going to bed without George. Still, I say out loud every night, "Goodnight, George. I love you. I miss you."

In my own life, I've known since age three how to lead a happy life. I enjoy myself, do what I love, and make a difference by helping people. I've done this before I recently discovered the book, *The 3 Promises: Find Joy Every Day. Do What You Love. Make A Difference*, by David J. Pollay. Pollay, a positive psychology expert and performance coach, suggests a complete strategy to be happy every day.

He says, "I've found that if you make three simple, daily promises to yourself, you can create a life filled with joy, personal and career satisfaction and the power to impact other people's lives positively. This is what truly leads to happiness." Pollay also wrote the international blockbuster, *The Law of the Garbage Truck*, that tells how to deflect negativity.

I still relish life every day. It's not anything unusual. I read a book or help my daughter or grandchildren on the phone with their challenges. I can't think of anything that gives me more pleasure in life than helping people. I've taught children and advised seniors, family, and friends for decades. I don't complain about my inadequate eyesight or difficulty walking. Life is terrific at age ninety-two.

Over the past half-century, I've changed for the better. I transformed from a mistake-prone, damaged person into someone more mature, trusting, positive, and happier than ever. I experienced a psychological understanding that I can find joy and happiness each day, no matter how tough the fight or big the worry.

I'm the worrywart grandma, too concerned about the well-being of my daughter and her kids. I'm bothered about my increased immobility, friends expiring, and health issues of my family. I recently fretted over the effort I'd need to travel and celebrate my birthday in Las Vegas with my daughter and granddaughter. But you know what? That's natural and common for anyone, especially us aging geezers. But these issues haven't prevented me from living a full, active, happy life. Mom always taught me not to worry constantly. That's easier said than done.

I had trust issues. In the 1960s, I was fearful of letting a man holding me by the ankles ten stories up in the air over the Blarney Stone. After I kissed the stone, I said out loud, "This was fun." I could now trust people I didn't know.

There's one thing that wasn't modified in my character over the years. I'm still a maverick, a rebel who does not conform to norms or established conduct. I've been busy redoing my house lately— replacing the floor, ceiling, window curtains, and roof. Neighbors suggest I replace my curtains with plantation shutters. That's what every-body does. I don't do what everybody does.

I created more meaning and insight into my life by finding joy every day, doing what I love and making a difference in peoples' lives. I did this on my own.

But now, a mysterious power has taken over my life. I'm curious how he will guide me the rest of the way.

[Page Intentionally Blank]

CHAPTER 16:
Life After Death?

I'm growing older. The worst thing for me about aging is my underarm flab! I'm ninety-two, and my doctor thinks I'll live for ten more years. Maybe longer.

In the 1990s, I finally reached age sixty-five and got my first gray hair. It was a decade of tremendous change. Mom died. Her precious life was ripped away from me. The Soviet Union fell, and the Internet rose. I cherished lifelong friends. I was thankful for the good life I had as I traveled to Asia. Terrorists attacked the World Trade Center, the Pentagon, and the Shanksville field.

Old age was a dangerous but exciting time to be alive. Just think, one year after I was born, sliced bread hit the market. I've seen the most exceptional innovations since sliced bread—televisions, microwave ovens, and personal computers. I used to put a nickel in my apartment payphone to talk to my girlfriend. Now I can find anyone or anything on my laptop or smartphone, call, text, or e-mail my friends and family and see and talk to them live on a screen and share pictures. All thanks to technological advances, including those in eye surgery and lenses.

I saw the most significant changes in the way people lived in the Twentieth Century since the start of civilization. I had what I desired most right at home—love and happiness with my husband George. Then it was taken away from me. George died in 2009. I lost something crucial to my existence. I tried to regain it, and live a joyful, productive life again. I didn't know whether I had the strength to do that. I couldn't immediately solve the breaking point. It threatened my survival. All I had left were memories and family.

Parental deaths left me with severe psychological wounds. I was not allowed to see Dad or Mom before they died. A couple decades after Dad died, I regretted not being able to say goodbye to Mom before she died. Mom spent her last month at the Selfhelp nursing home on Argyle Street. When she was hot and miserable, she asked me to take off her sweater. But I couldn't get it off. I asked a nurse to do it. I left Mom's room for a meeting about her care with the staff and my brother and sister.

After the meeting, I asked Morley and Shelly to go back to Mom's room with me and see if she was more comfortable then. They couldn't go. They had to get home to take care of kids. I pleaded with them, "Let's go back to see Mom." They ignored me. I rode with them, and we all went home. I didn't say anything to them on the way. I walked into my house, and the phone rang. The nurse said, "Your mom just died. I gave her something to help her rest. She fell asleep and died."

I think the nurse gave her a lethal dose of medication. But we never questioned it. We didn't go back to the nursing home. I never saw Mom again. I didn't see her in a casket. That's not the way I wanted to remember her. I regret—to this day—that I never got to kiss Mom goodbye before she died. Mom was eighty-eight years old and such a loving woman. I berated myself for not going back to see Mom. I didn't know it would be my last chance to see her alive.

The day came I prayed would never happen. George became seriously sick. He had trouble walking and fell a few times. Doctors found that he had water on the brain, an obstruction preventing fluid drainage. They were draining his mind, and an antibiotic-resistant superbug attacked the tube. The tube was removed, and George went steadily and uncontrollably downhill for months.

You never really know a man until he utters his last few words. That's when I discovered what was really important in George's life and who he really was.

Just before George fell into a coma at a hospice, he whispered into my ear, "I want you to go back to Florida, enjoy our condo and remarry." Holding his hand firmly and sniffling, I replied in a flirting tone, "Who would want an old lady like me?" Weeping, he softly spoke his last words: "I do."

It was surreal. Like he remarried me there. Tears poured down my cheeks. At 9:30 at night, George peacefully slipped away from me, assuredly forever at age eighty-four. I thought we were cheated out of a few more years together. But now I could only try to let go of him.

Memories of George are all I have left to keep me going.

He was a hero in World War II. At age 18, he graduated from high school, got his diploma, and draft notice on the same day! He was rushed into the war with little training. He found himself as his battalion's "point man" in the Battle of the Bulge, the decisive battle of the war. He was the first soldier in the most exposed position on an undermanned American front line.

In the 26th Infantry Division, my husband sacrificed his life and barely survived our country's deadliest battle of the war. The temperature plunged to minus four degrees Fahrenheit in the snowy Belgium woods.

He got peppered with shrapnel from head to toe and passed out. The enemy thought he was dead. When he came to, he walked on a painful broken leg and called for medics to help his buddies. His courage and determination and those in his unit helped stop Hitler's last-ditch strike.

CHAPTER 16 Life After Death?

George earned a Purple Heart and Bronze Star. He was hospitalized for six months. He had shrapnel all over his body; a broken jaw, leg, and arm; and a concussion.

At his military funeral, George's casket was draped with an American flag. A soldier played taps. Then the honor guard folded the flag into a triangle. A presenter knelt down in front of me, laid the banner on my lap, and said, "We appreciate his service."

I said quietly to him, "You'll never know what it cost him." I didn't say another word. I meant that I thought his extensive war injuries killed him.

Little things showed our love: Reaching over and touching George in bed. Holding hands at the theater. Watching the sunrise over a Florida beach. Sharing an ice cream sundae together. Now, as I pass his gift of a Chinese painting on my dining room wall, I think of him every day.

I worried about how I'd survive without George. Any time I thought of him, I quickly shed tears. I couldn't sleep, eat, or concentrate much. I depended on him to help me see, like a second pair of eyes. I couldn't go anywhere without him. He drove the car. The hardest part of life without George was not being able to share my feelings with him, not having sex with him, and not having him take out the garbage.

Our love grew every day—from platonic friends to red hot married lovers, well-suited for each other. George, if you're hearing this, your marriage proposal was so sincere, and I made you wait forty-three days for my answer. Isn't it odd: We were married for forty-three years. For each day you waited for me to answer your proposal, we were married for one year. If I had it to do over, I would say, "Yes!" without hesitating.

After I tearfully cleaned out George's stuff, I went to my Florida condo for the winter and a fresh start. I was going to start a new life successfully without him. At eighty-two, I was still a capable and competent woman with a positive self-image. But I'd need help. I'd have to rely on my tenacity, delivered groceries, and rides from neighbors to go anywhere.

For the first time, I entered my condo as a widow. I bawled bitterly, opening the front door. I was greeted by several inches of water on the floor! A water pipe under the foundation had broken. After the maintenance man removed the water, I sniffled myself to sleep. The next day, I was in a daze. All I could think about was how I missed George.

I was on my own and not near family in Illinois anymore. Traditions naturally fell. I was never very religious. I lived in a kosher home, and we celebrated Jewish holidays and Christmas and Easter. Mom always cooked a big Thanksgiving dinner; my daughter continues it.

I don't know how it started, but now a mystical, spiritual power controls my life. It guides me through life, encourages me to be positive, compassionate, and be a better person. It helps me feel better emotionally. And, hopefully, it may help me live even longer—at least until this book is published.

I hesitate to tell you this, but I have ghost stories and visits from the dead. I believe in God, and I'm convinced the spiritual power that controls my life is really my deceased husband. His spirit watches over me and guides my life.

I regularly see George, hear him, sense him, talk to him, and sometimes feel him gently touching my shoulder. I'm not crazy. This is all utterly normal and remarkably common, according to research studies. Singer Céline Dion revealed she still senses the presence of her late husband, can hear him, and talks to him too.

George is a dominant force that keeps me going every day. He's always with me spiritually, right here in my home. I feel George's presence daily, watching over me. If the girls do something amazing, I see him smiling. Granddaughter Amanda says she's felt his presence occasionally. "If I've got a problem, papa's there to help me," she told me. He gives her self-confidence in decisions ranging from men to work.

When I'm frustrated, I'll see George's face looking at me as he says, "Don't worry, it's going to be OK." He touches me once in a while. If I'm sad or concerned about something, he'll gently put his hand on my shoulder.

I even talk to him occasionally. One night in the middle of the summer of 2019, I couldn't sleep. I was feeling miserable and lonely, which rarely happens. My daughter had just left from visiting me. I don't know what came over me. But I had enough. With George standing right in front of me, I said, "I want to join you." In a forceful, angry voice, he replied, "No! Not yet." That was the end of the conversation. I'm glad he talked some sense into me.

As I left his burial ceremony, I saw George and heard him say to me, "I love you." I replied, "I miss you. I love you too." He then responded, "I'm all right. Don't worry about me. I love you." When I first entered my condo alone, I whimpered out loud, "This isn't fair. George, I love you and miss you." He said to me, "Go on with your life. I love you."

I thought I was creepy, sensing my deceased spouse. But I discovered it is surprisingly natural, rarely talked about, and little-studied by researchers.

Most sober, healthy grievers experience a comforting phenomenon called grief or bereavement hallucinations. When someone dies, they're not gone. They stay with us— in our hearts, minds, and our senses. You may see them as a peripheral shadowy illusion, hear them, smell them, and even touch them and feel their presence. This is often recognized as a helpful way to deal with grief.

As many as 60 percent of widows or widowers see or hear dead loved ones, reported University of Milan researchers in the *Journal of Affective Disorders*. Many in the study didn't tell friends who might think they're mentally ill. Other research suggests that grief hallucinations may indicate that there's life after death.

In a study of elderly Wales widows and widowers, 39 percent of the group continued to feel the presence of lost loved ones. Some 12–14 percent had seen them, heard their voices, or talked to them (with a feeling the dead spouse was listening). Only 3 percent felt their touch.

When you speak to a deceased spouse, you're more likely to be coping with widowhood than those who don't. More than two-thirds of studied widows found their hallucinations gave them spiritual and emotional strength and comfort, reduced feelings of isolation, and provided encouragement during demanding tasks.

During Hurricane Irma in 2017, George somehow kept my community and me safe. He died on the day the hurricane struck, September 9, but eight years earlier. Number nine is a lucky number in Chinese culture. I think something from my dear husband controlled our fate.

My daughter was upset that I wouldn't evacuate my home while the hurricane was approaching. My neighbors and friends were also staying. The storm finally hit us. The wind wailed. I was scared. I feared for my life. I thought this could be it, and I wouldn't be able to tell my life story. My cousin Joey, in his thirties, had to evacuate his mobile home. He rode out the storm with me, and he was afraid.

I heard George comfort me, "Hold on, you're going to be OK."

We were lucky we escaped the storm's eye but faced up to eighty-four miles an hour winds. Our community suffered extensive tree and roof damage. Good ole George—no kidding—was looking after me. I was safe, and just my roof leaked a little. Hurricane Irma caused sixty-five billion dollars of damage in Florida and elsewhere, the fifth-costliest Atlantic hurricane. What a way to remember my husband's death!

I believe a clear sign that George is still with me is that he helped find my most treasured pieces of lost jewelry. This is unusual but true.

Here's what happened once. The moment I got home from a concert, I noticed I lost the bluestone of the rare Alaskan tanzanite ring. George had given me the ring. Girlfriend Ettie, who drove me, tore her car apart looking for the stone. I looked everywhere in my house. A day later, Ettie said, "We're going back to the hall to look for it." I told her, "You're nuts. They've probably vacuumed it up by now." But we went back to the hall. The manager, Ettie, and I started looking row by row.

The manager soon came up to me, opened his hand, and said, "Is this the stone?" Flabbergasted, I said, "I can't believe it! Yes, this is it. How could this be." He explained that the stone didn't get vacuumed up by the cleanup crew. The gem was lodged uptight against a seat support.

CHAPTER 16 Life After Death?

I was surprised. Now tell me, why would I find this unless some mysterious force was helping me?

Most recently, Cousin Joey found my missing lavender jade gold ring while straightening up a closet for me. The closet gets heavy use. As Joey moved the fishing poles, the ring fell to the floor. Joey was amazed. I'm sure George directed Joey to the ring. I verbally thanked George immediately, and I saw his image smile back at me. I live to communicate with George's spirit.

I don't know if there is life after death. But this is evidence of something after you die. Naomi and Amanda believe George's spirit watches over me. When I lost the ring, they said, "Papa's going to direct someone to find it." George bought the ring for me in 1992 in Chiang Mai, Thailand. I wore it every day until it went missing for more than a year. The ring brought me good health and recharged my energy. I can't wait to get it resized and back on my finger. I think the ring kept me fit and active while traveling.

Long-distance travel is more difficult for me now. That's why I fretted many hours about going to Las Vegas with my family to celebrate my ninety-first birthday. Actually, we'd also be celebrating the birthdays of Naomi, fifty, and Amanda, twenty-five, all within a few weeks. Our ages spanned three-quarters of a century.

I thought there couldn't be a better place to celebrate my milestone among nonstop debauchery. I was sure there would be just enough excitement for me without embarrassing myself. I flew from West Palm Beach to Chicago, met Naomi and Amanda, and we traveled to Vegas first-class.

I don't gamble, but I enjoyed the stay in a fancy fifty-fifth-floor penthouse at the Palms Casino Resort. The suite had a huge, $10,000 two-door refrigerator in the ultra-modern kitchen and a hot tub on the balcony. On our last day, we stayed up half the night getting tattoos. The girls got firefly and feather tats. I didn't want one. But I ate one legal marijuana-loaded hard lemon candy and crashed for a peaceful nap.

I got up later, and the girls pleaded with me to do something even more outrageous and humiliating. They said, "You've got to do this. We want to be a threesome." I said, "OK, I'll only live once."

The three of us dyed our hair purple! I was out of my mind. My hair went from gray to fuchsia and violet or purple. I felt like a 55-year-old, ready to make my mark on The Strip. People stopped, smiled, and laughed at our three generations of purple hair. We fit in supremely with the wild, crazy atmosphere. I felt like I belonged in Sin City.

The Las Vegas adventure turned out to be a "trip" of a lifetime. (Pun intended). I lived like royalty and bonded with the girls like never before. When I got back to my 55-plus condo community with purple hair, residents called me "crazy" and "nuts." It was the most fabulous time I ever had with my family! I don't know what we'll do to top this next birthday. Maybe skydiving or bungee jumping. Ha!

Imagine me with purple hair and with my enigmatic personality that intrigues and confuses people. Plus, I already looked funny. I squint "like a sea captain steering through a gale" and read two inches from my brown eyes. I've dressed in eclectic clothes. I speak of my dead husband still touching me, finding lost jewelry, and protecting me from hurricanes.

I'm still kind of a flashy dresser upper. I love color and dress simply now. People look at me funny. They see me squinting to see better. If they ask me if I can see, I just give them the Clint squint. Actor Clint Eastwood does it to look more like a badass character. It gives my personality depth and makes me look wise.

George said I looked "lovely," and, ah, we lived the good life: theater, travel, food and drink, dancing and gifts. We weren't rich then, and I'm not rich now. We never had to worry about money. We both worked. I've lived comfortably, not affluently. Money, to me, means security. Money to Dad meant power.

I thanked God every day for my amazing life, even during the 2020 global coronavirus pandemic. I've never seen anything like it. No one has. Many people were worried and scared. They had negative thoughts. They feared losing everything they've worked for their entire lives, including money, food, and a roof over their heads. They thought of all the things that could possibly go wrong tomorrow and months into the future.

Life follows your thoughts. I advised my family and friends, "Think positively." That helped me and many others through these tough times. It gave us strength and power to survive. You should always find something to be grateful for. I'm thankful that I'm alive and healthy today, that I have a loving family and friends who watch out for me, and that I live in a great community and country. I concentrate on getting through each day with a healthy attitude and don't look ahead. I take life one day at a time.

During this crisis, I especially loved helping others on the telephone. I called friends and family members. I encourage them to do something at home other than watching television that makes them happy. I let them know I'm thinking of them and love them. God has helped us through tragedies and emergencies before, and he will again . . . if you have faith.

I'm fortunate. Normally, I'm still living the good life. I'm thrilled. I've got good health. I've got family and friends. I've got activities. I'm well fed. I always have something to do. I read novels and historical books, play Solitaire, wash clothes, cook, research on the computer or phone. If I go out with my walker, I'll go to theaters (including Metropolitan Opera broadcasts), restaurants, social events, and meetings. I still travel to see family, and recently played bocce and darts. My toughest decision every day is what I'm going to fix for dinner.

Once recently, though, I had a "full plate" of old agedness at the same time. My blood pressure was shooting through the roof. My granddaughter injured her knee playing field hockey, and I worried that she might need surgery. My roof leaked after a heavy rainstorm, damaging my ceiling. My air conditioning unit froze up, leaking water, and ruining my laminate floor. My air conditioning man said I needed a new system—$7,000. My condo assessed everyone $3,000 to put new roofs on some units. I worried so much I couldn't sleep.

You know how Mom said, "Tomorrow will always be a better day." It was! My doctor got my blood pressure down to normal. The condo repaired my roof temporarily. A good Samaritan neighbor got me an honest air conditioning man, and I didn't need a new system. My granddaughter didn't need surgery.

During all this commotion, I fell in my house, and I couldn't get up! Fortunately, I had a medical alert unit around my neck, and I called for help. The medics arrived 20 minutes later. I was still on the floor. They said I didn't need to go to the hospital. The best part was a medic made me a peanut butter and jelly sandwich for my dinner! I'm so grateful that a higher power watches over me.

I've had a problem with water leaks in my condo unit in the past 10 years. First, a not-turned-off toilet flooded the place while we were up North. I had to get all new furniture. The second, the under-the-foundation water pipe broke, requiring all new laminate flooring. I thought of the French expression, "Jamais deux sans trois," meaning what happens twice will surely happen a third time. It did. My dirty air conditioning filter sent water all over my laminate flooring recently. I spent thousands of dollars to install new flooring again. This time waterproof tile!

My family has always lived close to me and could help me if I need it. Morley, Shelly, and I once all lived in Florida near each other. When George's health started failing, we spent the winters at my brother's condo. Then we bought our own unit in the same Boynton Beach community, called Limetree, a quiet place with caring neighbors in Palm Beach County.

We moved in. A couple days later, I saw Morley and his wife Betty walking on our street. I rushed out of the house and asked Morley, "What are you doing here?" Morley said, "We live right over there," pointing to a unit just two doors down the street where we had stayed! Trying to laugh it off, I explained, "All the units looked the same to us."

Shelly and her husband Ray bought a condo unit that same year in the next town. We three kids united again and looked forward to many happy sibling reunions ahead!

CHAPTER 16 Life After Death?

Without George, I'm happy living alone in my two-bedroom condo. I live by myself like more than 40 percent of Americans without a spouse or partner. I'm not lonely. Many people who live by themselves are. We actually have a loneliness epidemic, and experts say it may be deadlier than obesity.

I like living alone. I can do whatever I want when I want. I can get up early or sleep late or nap. I can eat meals when I want. Like Mom, I never remarried after losing my husband. I couldn't go to bed with anybody else either. I still love George. In the morning, the first thing I say to myself is, "Thank you, God, for another good day." Then I keep doing what I love all day long. My worst fear is dying alone unexpectedly here without saying bye and telling my girls I love them. My family worries about me living alone.

I'm most happy about being ninety-two years old! I feel twenty years younger. The older I get, the better I feel. I'm active, healthy, and still a little attractive (I think). I'm the oldest of three living siblings or half-siblings; three are deceased. My secret of feeling younger is that I do rewarding things I can still do and don't focus on the hardships of aging.

As a result, I'm happier and healthier than even many teens and younger adults. I may live more than seven years longer than less optimistic people, says a scientific study. Lack of vision and my age never stopped me from leading a full life! Nothing stops me—not age, not blindness, not my black sheep childhood. Not injuries, crises, or death of loved ones. Just nothing stops me.

Pet dogs helped keep our family and me healthy and vibrant. They made our hearts stronger. Their deaths broke our hearts. My family always had a dog or two. We loved dogs. We gave Naomi, nine, her first dog, who looked like Benji and was named Muppet.

Years later, Naomi, a lover of animals, surprised George and me by giving us a chocolate Labrador called Hershey Big Block. Both dogs mainly competed for George's attention. Hershey put her head in George's lap, and Muppet jumped right into his lap. Muppet died at eighteen and Hershey, six, a few years later from a birth complication. We didn't have any more dogs because they broke our hearts.

I mended my heart with what I learned as an adult. If you have positive relationships with family and friends, you'll be physically healthier, less stressed, and likely to live longer, says the National Institutes of Health. My life is most meaningful helping shape the lives of my daughter and granddaughters with my lifetime of experience. I once helped change Amanda's life, advising her to find a more challenging job than being a waitress. She found a job at a Chicago securities brokerage and loved it.

After I give my kids advice, I can't sleep. I worry about them. I get insomnia, more common among the visually impaired. We don't get light clues from our eyes telling the brain, "It's time to sleep" and not to sleep.

I found that the phrase "Have faith" can be therapeutic. It inspired me in childhood, in my youth, and throughout my adult life. Just my name or the word "faith" has given many other people hope too. When something bad turns into something good, I've heard a person say, "I knew things would get better if I just had faith!" Another person will give hope to a troubled individual this way: "I'm so sorry you're going through such a tough time. Just have faith."

I sometimes use it myself: "Have faith, Arleen, that surgery will go well." Or if I'm around people, they might hear my cell phone ring tone song, *Faith* by George Michael (" . . . I gotta have faith . . . "), and they laugh.

I changed from being lost in life to being bigger than life. I only realized that as I wrote this book. My life story can be summed up in six words—legally blind but changed the world. For more than a half-century, my life's work has been to teach, motivate, and inspire people of all ages. . . from teaching children with disabilities to advising seniors with infirmities. I'll never stop helping people.

I've spread small acts of kindness everywhere—from Boynton Beach to Chiang Mai. They range from taking beggars for a sandwich to hugging strangers. What George wrote near his death brings tears to my eyes: "Loving, helping, sincere, giving all the time—that's my wife,

Faith. Bless her, may she continue forever to get pleasure so altruistically."

My unselfishness was triggered by the sage advice of Aunt Belle. I was ten years old, and she told me, "Travel is the best education."

CHAPTER 17:
Staying Grounded

O ld friends kept me grounded in thought but free to fly the world. I value them. They are part of my family.

"Old friends pass away, new friends appear. It is just like the days. An old day passes, a new day arrives. The important thing is to make it meaningful: a meaningful friend - or a meaningful day."

—Dalai Lama

I've known a group of my best friends since high school—almost eighty years. And we have a strong bond because of it. No one knows me better than them. They always have my back, and I have theirs. We love each other through thick and thin. Together we're strong, alone we're weak. We're just like a real family. In fact, better.

But now lifelong friends are dying one by one. How can I cope with losing them? I felt utterly normal with them. Now they're not there any longer.

I got along better with friends than with Dad and my family of origin. Families can be severe, harmful, and obligatory. Friends that I picked brought lightness, positivity, and a sense of security and value to my life.

As old friends die, I'm making many new friends where I now live. They have different interests and tastes, introduce me to other people, and broaden my perspective on life. New friends at my Limetree condo include Arleen, Sheila, Mary, Dina, and more. They check on me, take out my garbage, and drive me where I want to go. You just can't find this kindness anywhere.

My greatest joy is talking to old and new friends. There's nothing that satisfies me more than hearing Ettie or another friend on my smartphone. I speak to Ettie, my closest living friend from high school, on my cell phone every day. Ettie and my other close friends have helped me be happier, healthier, and live longer. Good friends are there for each other.

One day my iPhone mysteriously locked up, and I couldn't use it. I panicked. It's a vital communication tool for me. My whole life is in there—my friends, photos, documents, doctors, everything and more. I couldn't call out or receive calls. Neighbors were knocking on my door to see if I was OK.

Chapter 17 Staying Grounded

Sheila, a neighbor across the street, took me to a store, and the techie cleared the problem. I was fortunate not to lose any data, which was automatically backed up to the cloud. I couldn't live without the information. My phone is my mind. Unlike many people my age, I'm not afraid of technology, either on my iPhone or computer. It's a blessing and my friend. But I can't stand when it doesn't work right.

I've been active in my condo community. I started its book club. I've chaired a Chinese dinner party, been a member of the social committee, go to its theater outings, and have played bocce. I made a big decision to play a friendly game of darts in the Activities Building. Could I hit the target with my fuzzy eyesight? I really didn't want to go. But close friends would be there to socialize. I needed to be ready to play, though. I watched a video on how to throw a dart-like a pro.

Sheila drove me to the dart game. My last throw was typical of my results. I walked towards the dart-throwing line. More than twenty friends cheered me on. "Come on, Faith, you can do it," encouraged Sheila. Sweat spread over my palms. I planted my toes behind the throwing line. I heard my racing heartbeat echoing in my ears, lub-DUB, lub-DUB, lub-DUB. I squinted my eyes, like I usually do, to try to see better.

I grasped the corrugated Tungsten barrel between my thumb and forefinger, cocked my arm at the elbow, briefly eyed the target, and closed my eyes. Then I hurled the dart with all my strength, wobbling through space at fifty miles an hour. I heard a faint thud ninety-six inches away. I opened my eyes. The players loudly uttered, "Ohhhhhhs." Surprise. The steel-tipped dart hung precariously in the dartboard.

Don announced my feat with a quivering shout, "Oneeeee point." "Yeah," I whooped loudly. "I got one point for my team." Everyone applauded. "Nice going, Faith," Tom said. That was my last throw. Sadly, the twenty-six other darts I threw missed the target completely. Getting one point was a miracle. The target was one big blur to me. My dismal performance was OK. I was just there to get out and mix with neighbors. Yet, I was a success. I pushed myself to try something new. I didn't give up after failing initially. I did what I wanted to do, regardless of my showing or what people said about me.

Friends are a significant part of my life. I wouldn't be here without them. They're my biggest source of support and comfort. And I'm fortunate to have had many friends. But my closest friends are dying, getting very sick, or disappearing. I have a group of most intimate friends, faithful companions who are like a family. They are my high school group known as The Circle. Five of seven of them are still living: Ettie, Evie, Ellie, Claire, and me.

Esther died from liver cancer in 2013. I was lucky to have her as an incredible friend for seventy-seven years.

She was my literary foil. Sight-impaired like me, she was short and chunky compared to my tall, thin frame. We were both smart and off-the-wall. Another good friend, Elaine, I just found on Facebook after searching for her for five years. That was so exciting to see she was alive.

Several friends and family members call me for faith and support. I'm a faith healer! Not a traditional one. I treat their situation with common sense and wisdom. Friends call me when they have love problems or loved ones die or get sick with cancer or other diseases. My girl-friend from Minnesota just called, and we talked for an hour. She got fired from her job the same day she learned her husband has Alzheimer's. I advised her, "Enjoy your time with him and accept him where he is now."

Growing evidence suggests that faith may keep us well. Faith includes believing in a loving God, praying, meditating, spirituality, or going to religious services. Even fasting has health benefits. All across the world and faiths, many people believe a spiritual power can heal ill-nesses. Extensive research indicates that people who are more religious and pray more are healthier.

I found that I've been happy and healthy with strong ties to my family and to friends. People need people. But I discovered that friends are more critical as I age. I kept friends that made me feel good and dropped others that didn't.

PART 3 REBIRTH JUST IN TIME

Studies have found that friends are better predictors of health and happiness than family. You're stuck with your family, who may cause health troubles. Research shows that friendships influence daily happiness and longevity more than relationships with spouses and family.

Every time I lose an old friend, I'm devastated for weeks. The only thing I can do is make new friends and keep busy. I don't get around much, so I've made friends with neighbors in my community. You're never too old to make new friends. Here are a few quick tips for meeting new friends: (1) Accept invitations, (2) Go to senior centers, (3) Attend events of your own interests, (4) Invite neighbors for dinner, and (5) Get a dog.

I've traveled extensively with friends. Traveling is exciting. But it can be dangerous too. It's fun, exhausting, and risky. I was in it for the joy (and shopping), without thinking much about the perils. George and I exposed ourselves to crime, accidents, immigration issues, problems at home, and our own health and sanity. We took risks, then conquered our fears. We faced crises and needed to get home safely.

Aunt Belle encouraged me to travel, saying, "See how other people live . . . You'll appreciate being an American . . . after you've gone places." I had to find out for myself. After three decades of travel, what I found was shocking and heart-stopping.

226

Chapter 17 Staying Grounded

I was passionate about traveling around the world and planned all our trips. I, or both George and I, went to thirty countries in Asia, Europe, and North America. Each trip kindled my desire to see more of the world. I was overly ambitious scheduling an Asian tour. We got exhausted taking sixteen planes in twenty-four days. Never again!

I often got an idea to travel someplace. I'd ask George. This is how the conversation usually went:

— *"How about going to China? Our friends say it's so wonderful."*

— "You're out of your head!"

— *"But, George, you know we've got the money to do it."*

George, pauses while thinking, not wanting to lose control over me but giving in:

— "Well, if you want to."

That's what he always said, "If you want to." He never said, "No," on any of my trip ideas, though. Once we started a trip, he'd say, "I'm glad we did this. This is so interesting."

Or when I asked George to go to Hawaii:

— *"George, I would really love to see Hawaii."*

— "You've got to be kidding. That's too expensive."

— *"Well, George, I found a tour to the four islands that's very reasonable. Let me tell you about it . . ."*

— "That sounds very interesting, Faith. I think we can do it."

And we did. Many times.

PART 3 REBIRTH JUST IN TIME

I saw my "old" school friends, sometimes when I visited Chicago. I take tedious trips back to Chicago to see my daughter and granddaughters a couple times a year. My daughter makes a fantastic Thanksgiving dinner, and the kids are so damn loving, sweet, and hospitable on Mother's Day.

Single friends and I would often travel together. Once Ettie, Barbara, and I went to Mexico City. We stayed at the Sheraton Mexico City Maria Isabel Hotel. I noticed some duct tape every so often across the floor. I thought they were doing some repair work.

One night we were sound asleep in our suite on the tenth-floor. Suddenly, our room started swaying like tree leaves in the wind. Someone in the hall screamed, "Earthquake. Get out!" We helped each other evacuate, wearing raincoats and carrying our contact lenses and checkbooks. I said, "Please, dear God, not here!" We were unhurt. Some thirty-two people were killed. It was a big earthquake.

We girls were shaken, nauseous, and oddly hungry for steak. After that, I bought an eighty-dollar gold bracelet to soothe my nerves, with a loan from a kind friend. As Dionne Warwick sang, "For good times and bad times, I'll be on your side forevermore, that's what friends are for."

Our Block family spent a lot of time in Hawaii. We all fell in love with the islands. I adored Maui with its beautiful coastline, but George and Naomi fell for Oahu with Honolulu and its beautiful trails and epic surfer waves.

We all went back to Hawaii several times, where we celebrated special family occasions, with as many as seven family members for as long as two weeks.

I always loved big celebrations of special events, like birthdays or anniversaries. We celebrated our eighteenth wedding anniversary in Honolulu and were joined by Esther. We had a cocktail on the roof of the Outrigger Waikiki, watched the sunset, and then George and I took a dinner cruise.

My plan was to seduce George into bed that night. I wore a long sexy tight, low-cut red dress. I described it as simple elegance. It was tight in the parts that should be tight and loose at the parts that should be loose.

After dinner, we danced all night under the stars—well not quite all night, ahem . . .

We were both incredible dancers and were always the last couple off the dance floor. We danced to everything, even cha-chas and meringues. If I didn't know a step, George led me through it. I could dance with anybody, except for out-of-step Dad at my wedding. George loved the fast stuff, I liked the slow mushy music, like our favorite dance song, *Lara's Theme from Dr. Zhivago*. Where did the evening go? After the last dance, George looked me in the eyes and said, "Well, that's it." I said, "Too bad. Tomorrow's another day." Time to go to bed . . .

While visiting Esther in Santa Monica, we drove to see the Baja Peninsula in Ensenada. On the way back before we crossed from Mexico into the U.S., I saw a man at the border selling a leather bag that I wanted. Our car was stopped in line at the crossing.

Esther gave money to seventeen-year-old Naomi, and she jumped out of the car and ran to the vendor. Meanwhile, customs officials motioned our car, driven by George, forward and across the border without Naomi. George tried to tell authorities that Naomi was a pedestrian, without identification or money, on the Mexico side. I was hysterical, ranting, and raving, trying to get someone to understand my story. Finally, someone did, and we were reunited with Naomi, who tells people that we "abandoned" her in Mexico. But she did get my leather bag!

George wasn't around to control me on another trip. I traveled to Cancún, Mexico, with Naomi. We went to a young people's nightclub, Señor Frog's. I don't know how much we had to drink, but Naomi challenged me.

At nearly sixty, I found myself dancing on a table! Everyone around me was clapping like I was the star of the evening. I would never do this ordinarily. Naomi, who was hysterical, got up on the table too. I don't usually dance the night away like this on a table.

I went to Israel in 1989 with Shelly. George couldn't leave teaching his class. A hired guide took our group to the Dead Sea, a salt lake between Israel and Jordan, and to Masada, a famous archaeological and Jewish religious site.

Chapter 17 Staying Grounded

Our guide said, "Don't stay in the water for too long. It will make you giddy." I wasn't a kid. I was sixty-two, but—as you probably guessed—I didn't follow his advice. I and others with me got very silly and laughed until our bellies hurt.

Friends told us how fascinating China was and how it was so different from our country. That was enough for me to start planning a trip to China. George and I got on a group tour. We were looking forward to seeing all the fabulous tourist attractions, like the Great Wall of China.

Our tour bus got lost, and we were horrified seeing the hidden, worst poverty in China! Even though conditions were improving in the early 1990s, we saw masses of homeless adults and children without food and water. This made me realize how fortunate I was to be living in the United States and how I didn't value my good life. I learned to appreciate what I had.

In the mid-1980s, George, Naomi, and I flew out to visit Esther in Santa Monica, California. We drove to Mexico and then San Francisco. We did all the busy sight-seeing stuff—walked the hills, bought tie-dyed shirts, and ate at the Top of the Mark. George complained of feeling tired, shortness of breath, and of indigestion. Thinking it was the food he ate, we ignored it and, as scheduled, headed back to Evanston that night.

The next morning, George was cold and clammy, a heart attack sign I knew from training at work. Naomi drove him to the hospital. I told an attendant that he was having a heart attack. He was rushed into the hospital and had open-heart surgery.

George's doctor told me, "You saved his life." He recovered successfully.

My last trip with George, hobbling but too independent to use a scooter, was to Vancouver, Canada. It was after an Alaska cruise. For a guy who hesitated to travel, George was a travel trouper until near the end of the road. For my eighty-first birthday, he romanced me with a fancy sunset dinner. It was on the forty-second floor of the torn-down Empire Landmark Hotel's Cloud Nine restaurant, with revolving 360-degree views of Vancouver. He died a year later at age eighty-four.

Travel took me out of my comfort zone. Not only did I discover the world, but I also found myself. You're happy in a routine. You have little stress and risk. Sometimes you need to break out of your comfort zone. Do things you fear doing, such as river rafting. You'll be more productive, more creative, and more able to deal with future uncertainties. I escaped daily stress by traveling extensively.

Travel broadened my view of the world. Life came so easy for me. The more I traveled, the more I appreciated what a beautiful life I have here in this country. I curiously discovered new places and people, even off the beaten path. But I also learned new things about my inner life and worldview. The farther and oftener I traveled—ran away from myself—the closer I got to me.

Trips strengthened our marriage and transformed my life. Travel shed light on my fear, confidence, tenacity, love, curiosity, and view of poverty. I was more open and romantic with George than at home. I felt closer to him and loved him more each day. If I hadn't traveled to Hawaii and China with George for an extended period, I might never have realized the strength of our relationship.

I saw him at his best and worst on the road. The ultimate test of love is seeing someone at his worst and still loving him just as much. George cut his leg and was at his worst. We argued over where to get medical treatment.

If I hadn't traveled to China and Thailand, I would not have seen firsthand the extreme struggle of needy people. I become more compassionate of all underprivileged people. My time in Ireland taught me that even though I am tenacious, I can't always win. I couldn't wait out lousy weather long enough to see the Gap of Dunloe.

Travel was fun and exciting. I don't travel much anymore. But trips abroad changed my life significantly. I'm less fearful of heights and confide in strangers more. I'm healthier, less stressed, more creative, happier, and have a lower risk of depression, all proven health benefits of foreign travel.

PART 3 REBIRTH JUST IN TIME

Yet, my evolution as a person is not complete. A painful, dark secret threatens to destroy what is most important to me . . .

CHAPTER 18:
A Nostalgic Crisis

You have seen how I overcame legal blindness in childhood, Dad's black sheep snub as a teen, and rebirth in marriage. I found happiness in all these challenges.

In my golden years, I'm now up against a more significant test that threatens my contentment again. A sad secret exploded in the past few years, threatening what's most important to me.

Over my nine decades, I've learned how to find joy and taught many people to enjoy life more. I've passed my legacy of positivity and faith in a letter to family and friends.

It's not easy to find pleasure every day. Here are some thoughts on how I did it.

I could have gone into a severe depression when my husband died. Instead, I let other people help me. I interacted with positive people. And I did something I loved to do. Reading. Talking to family and friends. Going to the theater. That was my secret to being happy every day.

I enjoy life more than ever.

Mom taught me to be happy every moment of every day. I discovered an attitude, as expressed by the late J. Donald Walters (aka Swami Kriyanda), an authority on meditation and yoga:

> *"Happiness is an attitude of mind, born of the simple determination to be happy under all outward circumstances."*

I've always been happy, strong-willed, and unwavering. My strength of character made up for lack of a natural advantage—healthy eyesight. I'm in control of what happens every moment. I seek new challenges so I can grow and take risks that most other people would never do.

I've been doing three things that researchers say increase enjoyment in seniors—being more thankful, generous, and positive. I thank God every day for giving me such a beautiful life. That alone improves physical and psychological health and gives me a positive outlook. I've always been generous with time and money for deprived and disease-stricken people, particularly cancer and diabetes victims. Whether alone or with family and friends, life couldn't be better.

I've been a motivational leader—educating kids, counseling the elderly, and advising my daughter and granddaughters. My goal is to educate and encourage everyone to be productive and happy at all times. I look forward every day talking to family and friends, helping them with something that matters to them.

I don't settle for mediocrity. I always try to get something extra out of life. Make time more enjoyable. Go against the grain. Do something wild and silly (dying my hair purple). I'm a maverick at heart. Yet, I think I transformed myself into someone worth knowing. Every day is an exciting, new beginning, guided by the spirit of my husband always at my side. With his approval, I am writing my legacy letter to all readers, especially my family.

> *"The greatest legacy one can pass on to one's children and grandchildren is not money or other material things accumulated in one's life, but rather a legacy of character and faith."* —Billy Graham

Dear Readers

(Especially my daughter, Naomi and granddaughters, Amanda, Kaylee, and Chloe, plus family, friends and neighbors),

I am writing to you because I want you to know I am 92 years old, very healthy, and not dying. This is an excellent place to pass on and preserve life's lessons for present and future generations. For me, *It's A Wonderful Life*, as in the classic 1946 Christmas movie. Remember, guardian angel Clarence shows businessman George Bailey (played by Jimmy Stewart) how the world would be worse off had he never been born. What if I had never been born? Would the world be worse off without me?

George put his dreams on hold to help others in need. I postponed my dreams of being a teacher to help people get back on their feet after World War II. I showed them how to buy homes, furniture, and cars. If I had never been born, many needy people would have suffered longer.

George and his wife Mary (Donna Reed) toasted a new homeowner: "Bread, that this house may never know hunger. Salt, that life may always have flavor. And wine, that joy and prosperity may reign forever." This was also the sentiment of my life—true worth is measured in friends and family, not dollars. If I had not been born, my friends and family, I don't think, would experience as much joy.

George learned that the good he did affected other people. His life had a purpose. As a teacher and counselor, I helped change the lives of children and adults and made the world better. If I had never been born, many people would not have reached their full potential.

The sign in the office of Pa Bailey, George's father, said, "All you can take with you is that which you've given away." It means what you've done for others will live forever. I put the needs of family and friends before my own. If I had not been born, people around me would not have been able to grow and prosper.

After George married right-under-his-nose Mary in the movie, she stuck with him through all the good and bad times. My George (a name coincidence) stuck with me for 43 years, through thick and thin. If I had never been born, I could not have helped George become a better, more productive person and teacher because each person's life "touches so many other lives."

I feel I've helped change the world. I discovered my mission in life. For more than a half-century, my life's work has been to make people better. That was my calling. I've become the person I was always meant to be. I care more about other people's well-being than my own. I was never afraid of failing; it's one of the best teachers in life. I have faith in good luck and miracles because a powerful force watches over me.

These are the most important things I learned in life. If you do them, you'll be happier, live longer, be healthier than if you didn't:

Find joy every day. Do what you love. Help others.

I strongly believe in a higher being. Without spirituality, I'd never have discovered my husband's powers to guide my life.

How will you live your life? When I started living, I couldn't see. Now, at 92, my eyes are wide open to the world. I have a legacy of positivity. I'm invigorating the lives of people around me. My gift is being a good mother and grandmother to my girls. My life is my legacy. My calling is about helping people and bettering the world. I hope I can touch people for years to come. I'm not going anywhere soon. I'm sticking around to see my granddaughters grow. I'm happy. I wouldn't change anything in my life. My life is worth living, remembering and continuing . . . as long as I keep feeling like 72.

PART 3 REBIRTH JUST IN TIME

To my readers, I bless you with all my love. To my family and friends, I love you beyond words; you've been vital in my life. I wish you all health, happiness, and faith.

Faithfully yours,

Faith Block

Boynton Beach, Florida
April 16, 2020

I hope my sister reads my legacy letter. I love Shelly, and we were destined for closeness. We've hung out together since childhood. She is the only remaining family member that shares my childhood and adult memories. We now live near each other in Florida, making possible many happy reunions. I've had a long history of instinctively taking care of others and making them feel loved.

For more than eighty years, Shelly and I shared many warm and poignant moments. I protected her. As my baby sister, I nurtured her. We played with dolls and shared a bedroom. She watched my back. Shelly wanted to do my sewing.

We laughed together about her not bathing before a school photo. We cried together over Mom's stillbirth. We consoled together at our parents' divorce. We shared special occasions and trips—my wedding (she was my maid of honor), Christmas Day dinners at her house, and a trip to Israel. Her six young kids often got up early to open

Christmas presents. For five years, I was the one sleeping on the couch and charged with sending them back to bed.

Shelly and I often talked and laughed together, taking classes, attending a singles group, going to theaters and movies, and eating out. When her kidney was removed, she insisted I be at her side. Shelly and I endured uncertainty and pain together. I would die for her if I had to.

Dad would have been proud of Shelly and me as adults. At Mom and Dad's divorce, we promised him we would "love each other and stay close no matter what." This was our verbal blood oath that couldn't be broken. It was one of the most essential things in my life. We didn't know it then, but active ties to both family and friends would help keep us happy and healthy for a long time. As adults, we enjoyed our sisterly intimacy until . . . something happened. Then my world was turned into a profound disorder.

After more than 80 years, sis won't talk to me anymore in a friendly sisterly way. This is my disturbing family secret—I have a blood enemy. I disclosed this to a few friends. I've tried to communicate with Shelly many times in a loving sisterly way. For more than three years, she has tried to avoid me. I've called her and emailed her many times, especially around Thanksgiving, Christmas, and her birthday.

She usually doesn't respond. This shocks me. I recently reached her a couple times on the phone. But they were strained conversations. We didn't make up.

Our estrangement was not resolved.

I want us to be loving sisters who can talk freely and go out to lunch once in a while. I'm still hoping she still will want to end our separation forever and have a closer relationship.

Shelly had an incident with Family Services concerning her son, who lives with her. She thinks I had something to do with it. I did not. Shelly said, "I won't have anything to do with you because of this."

We used to be friends. It pains me to write about our sister strife. I needed to solve my sister estrangement, one of my most significant challenges of all. My last family crisis. Lack of vision and age have never stopped me from getting my way until now. I don't want to end our relationship this way in the twilight of our lives. I've lost nights of sleep over it, with tears pouring. It's something I won't take to my grave. This can't be the end of an age full of nostalgia and sisterly camaraderie.

Most sibling estrangements build for years, often from competing for parental affection from childhood. We fought for everything as kids. But we were completely different.

Shelly had a strong bond to Dad, more durable than her relationship with Mom, and was a spoiled brat. I was mama's girl and the family's black sheep.

I sense that Shelly today may resent or be jealous of me.

I was close to Morley. She was not. I married a man who gave me a good life. She did not, in my judgment. My daughter has a remarkable life, a lovely house, and children doing well. She has children I've seen that I think are not doing as well. I believe I may have had an easier time becoming successful in life than she did. She was an accomplished bank executive. I'm living by myself and don't need a caregiver. She has a live-in daughter that helps her. I'm thin, and she's heavier.

Shelly isn't the only one not talking to me. Her six children don't communicate with me. And I haven't heard a word from my five nephews and nieces, Mort and Betty's kids. I spent a lot of time taking them to circuses, ballets, concerts, and teaching them about art and music. Nephew Marty said I gave him the appreciation of arts and music. But I don't hear from any of them. I loved these kids, and they think I don't exist anymore. It's a shame. It turns out that blood is not always thicker than water in our Brickman family.

I've done everything to regain my childhood rapport with Shelly. The conflict became more personal, bitter, and devastating. I was up against two encounters—an external clash with a person and an internal battle with my mind.

PART 3 REBIRTH JUST IN TIME

When someone asks me, "How's your sister doing?" I just lie, "Great." I really do love her and miss her, but I don't want to talk about her to other people. Sibling estrangement is surprisingly common and one of the most painful human experiences. We're almost entirely estranged, estimated at 5 percent of American adults. It's a widely ignored problem. Parents and grown children morally want to stay in touch. But without reasons to reconcile, some people just say, "Screw it."

A few years ago, I thought Shelly was warming up to me. She went out of town, and I agreed to board their cat. Shelly dropped the cat off and picked it up, saying only a few words about the care of the cat. After she left with the cat, I let out a sharp scream that neighbors could hear. We had no meaningful conversation. I'm troubled over why things happened that way.

I sent my sister this message around Thanksgiving 2018: "I would like to end this estrangement for our sake and our families'. What would it take from me for you to agree to put this behind us?" I heard nothing back! So sad. There's nothing I can do except keep trying.

I've done everything to get her back. I've regularly tried to speak to her at family gatherings, by phone, and through e-mail. I tell her I love her and that I miss her. But she doesn't pay much attention to me. This is so frustrating. I replay these scenes over and over in my head, obsessing over them.

CHAPTER 18 A Nostalgic Crisis

I sometimes see her at the Metropolitan Opera live broadcasts in a local movie theater, but she ignores me. Just last week, we accidentally met face-to-face in the ladies' room at the theater. I asked, "Can I give you a hug? I miss you. Would that be difficult?" We hugged. I was surprised that she did that. I thought she might be willing to forgive me. I said, "Can we be friends?" Before I could apologize and promise a fresh start, she angrily replied, "No. I can never trust you," and she hurriedly walked out of the bathroom.

I was disappointed as tears flooded my eyes. Sometimes it takes time to reconcile with a sister. She may not be ready for it now. I pray that Shelly and I can make up.

Shelly, if you are reading this, I formally apologize for any pain you think I caused. I sincerely regret this incident. I genuinely love you and miss you in my life. I do not want us to harbor anger over this. I want to have a closer relationship with you for our sake and for the rest of our families. I want us to start fresh. What would we each have to do to talk to each other like loving sisters again? Shelly, will you accept my heartfelt apology and be willing to start fresh? I look forward to hearing from you. Please, please contact me now!

I made a decision that was inevitable (to me) and unexpected (to you). I decided to make up with my sister directly, no matter what it took. Most people, research shows, would be willing to reconcile if they got an apology and the promise of a fresh start. I planned to apologize to her in person, even if I did nothing wrong, and pledge to put this disagreement behind us. This will give both of us peace of mind before it's too late.

I found that you can't always fix a broken relationship or do it quickly. I've tried my best. It hasn't worked. I feel like a failure. My mood is mixed with sadness and nostalgia. Nothing lasts forever. Yet, I'll always leave the door open for her.

> *"Blood is thicker than water, so the fact that I have my sister always with me, it's like you always have someone who's your best friend and always have someone who has your back. You can always trust your family, and I'm lucky to have that."* —**Brie Bella**

My sister and I are still not talking as of this moment. But I believe she wants to be with me in spirit if not in fact. Fixing a broken sister relationship is harder than I ever imagined. I labored to resolve the crisis, but I haven't yet. Then again, I have not failed. I'm still trying. I have faith Shelly will come around someday—hopefully soon. This situation is out of my hands now. I've done my part. I think divine intervention will finally determine the outcome. Every day I look forward to a new and different life and sharing it with Shelly.

If nothing is working, experts advise cutting ties. That alone will significantly improve the overall quality of life.

But I won't do that. I'm living a good life and dreaming for more. I envision that my sister and I passed through all the possible obstacles separating us: distance in ages, childhood squabbles, parental attention, and sister estrangement. Now, we're hugging and commiserating each other like the world will end tomorrow. That's my dream.

But my story doesn't end, "And they lived happily ever after." My story doesn't end on a downer, either—unhappy, sad, or tragic. For now, it ends somewhere in between. It's a bittersweet ending. Shelly and I still cannot fully enjoy our unforgettable memories together.

This story, for me, still ends on a high note. I remain happy every day, healthy, and full of trying to make peace. I evolved as a person on my journey from overcoming my inner demon (legal blindness) to making life better for anyone. But my success came at a heavy price, mixed with sadness and nostalgia. I found peace and joy and happily live every day, knowing that I have helped many people live better lives.

I sleep well at night with my senses, knowing tomorrow will be another better day. Then I can cheerfully say, "I opened two presents this morning. They were my eyes." Thank you, God, for another great day.

[Page Intentionally Blank]

PART 4:
LIFE LESSONS

[Page Intentionally Blank]

CHAPTER 19:
Life Lessons

This section contains the best lessons I've learned in life. Use them to help improve yours. Each lesson is related to a specific chapter. The self-contained topics are designed to give lessons and short background material from other parts of the book in context. The information is based on my experience and research.

What to Do If Your Baby Is Visually Impaired (Chapter 3)

Blind and visually impaired children can lead happy and healthy lives. But parents must help every step of the way. Assistance is now available from many providers and services, unlike the few I had when I was a baby and toddler.

Parents of blind or visually impaired babies should:
- Cuddle the baby to learn to love each other, even though the baby can't make eye contact with you.
- Realize the baby may not cry when she wants your attention. She might be quiet, listening for you to be near her.
- Tell the baby what you're doing around her and what's within and beyond her reach.
- Let the baby touch people and objects.
- Treat the baby as a healthy child, talking to her, tickling her, or kissing her, for example.
- Socialize the baby with children and adults outside the home.
- Visit the American Foundation for the Blind's webpage, Resources for Parents of Children Who Are Blind or Visually Impaired (www.afb.org/blindness-and-low-vision/family connect-8160), for support, camaraderie with other parents, and local resources.

Visually Impaired/Blind Services (Chapter 3)

Here are some organizations that offer programs and services for the visually impaired and the blind (low vision to no vision):
- American Foundation for the Blind (https://www.afb.org/)

- Blinded Veterans Association
  https://www.bva.org/
- Lighthouse International
  http://www.lighthouseguild.org/
- National Federation of the Blind
  https://www.nfb.org/

Wonderland's Wonderful Lessons (Chapter 4)

This a treasure trove of advice that I learned from the book and movie *Alice in Wonderland*. I brought them into my real life, realizing that my scary unknowns were not as bad as I expected.

Believe the Impossible's Possible

"The only way to achieve the impossible is to believe it is possible," preached Alice's father in the movie. I was legally blind from birth, refused to learn Braille, and had fourteen eye surgeries. I believed I could do anything an average person could do, except seeing as well. I did, and I became a teacher.

Accept Your Flaws

Accept your defects, move ahead, and live your life fully. In the movie, Alice tells The Mad Hatter, "You're entirely bonkers. But I'll tell you a secret. All the best people are." To succeed, you have to be a little bit crazy. I wore eclectic clothing, ran under high-flying kids on swings, and dyed my adult hair purple. As an elementary school teacher and adult counselor, I changed the world.

Stick to Your Beliefs

Stick to your ideas, no matter how difficult it is. Not one of Dad's kids stood up to Dad, except me. I refused his request to take a relative on a trip and turned down his money to return to college. I learned to think for myself and do things my way, even if it was the hard way. This enriched my life tremendously.

Be Curious, Even Impulsive

Be curious yet spontaneous. I was curious like Alice when she followed the White Rabbit down the rabbit hole. I had an insatiable interest in the world, people, and cultures. I traveled to thirty countries, including a spontaneous trip to China, and was thankful I lived in the United States.

Look for A Way Out Right Away

If you fall down a rabbit hole, look for a way out right away. Don't just stay there or lament, "Woe is me." Sometimes you have to fall into a rabbit hole to figure out where you need to be. You may discover how to fix what's wrong in your life. I found a way out. Visually impaired, I did everything healthy children and adults did, just not as quickly.

Take Another Path

Alice believed there just isn't one way to get to where you need to go. If you get lost on one road, try another. If you're determined, you'll get there one way or another. I got lost trying to graduate from college, wandered a bit for sixteen years on a work path, but eventually earned a college degree.

Enjoy Life's Wild Journey

Enjoy life's wild adventure. Expect a roller-coaster-like range of emotions—joy-sadness, anger-fear, trust-distrust, and surprise-anticipations. The experience will make you a better person. I feared going on a roller coaster with my brother on my tenth birthday. Afterward, I got sick to my stomach. But I became a tougher person. I actually enjoyed the next roller coaster adventure with him.

Be More 'Muchier'

In the movie *Alice in Wonderland*, Alice, now age nineteen, returns to her childhood magical world. The Mad Hatter tells Alice that since her first visit, she's lost her "muchness." He thought Alice lost some of her childhood self—including bravery, courage, and enthusiasm. It's common to lose some muchness as you age, mature, and gain responsibilities.

Try to get some of your childhood muchness, innocence, and imagination back. Identify the essence of who you were and why you may have stopped doing things you loved as a kid. If you do some things you lost, I think you might be much happier, more positive, and muchier.

I discovered I still have my core childhood beliefs, attitudes, and values. I always do the things I liked to do as a kid: Eat sweets, read, and write. I've never really grown up. I'm still iron-willed, liberated, self-disciplined, and nurturing like I was as a child. That's why I think I'm so happy and content today because of my beliefs.

Be More Positive

Despite being almost completely blind, I've always been an incredibly positive person. Mom taught me positivity when I was three years old. Throughout life, my mantra has been, "Nothing stops me."

Be happier and more successful in life by letting other people's "garbage"—negativity—"pass by," says positivity expert David J. Pollay. Do not dump garbage on others. Pollay is the author of the bestselling book, *The Law of the Garbage Truck: How to Stop People from Dumping on You*. If you think optimistically, you are more likely to be successful in your personal and business lives.

I've discovered some effortless ways you can be more positive in your life. You should:

- Be more grateful. List the things in life that you are thankful for.
- Stand up straight.
- Be around positive people.
- Find two positive thoughts or gratitudes for every time you catch yourself thinking negatively.
- Smile more. When you get up, start your day by smiling, no matter what you're thinking. It's incredible how this tricks your mind into being positive all day long. Smile at everyone you see.
- Be kind to one or more people each day. Give someone a hug (if socially acceptable), show kindness to friends and family, or help someone less fortunate than you.

Find the Courage to Face Life

Alice and I both found the courage to face life. Alice found her bravery when the Queen threatened to silence her. She stood up to the Queen, proclaiming that all the Queen had were cards.

I, too, dared to find the nerve to stand up for myself to Dad. I refused his desire for me to take his sister-in-law on a trip. I was shocked when he praised me for standing up to him, adding I was just like him.

Learn from Failure

Failure is one of your best teachers. You become stronger from adversity. I discovered I needed to grow up. Make mistakes, get lost, get stuck, and get hurt a little. When I dropped out of college, I became stronger mentally. I worked until I had enough money to finish college—more than a dozen years later.

Be a Different Person Today

Be a different, better person today. I made a lot of typing mistakes working for Dad. He made me type documents over if they contained errors. I'd go to work the next day and not dwell on yesterday's mistakes. But I learned from them. Alice said, "I'm a different person today than yesterday." The lesson is that you should grow as you age, not be the person you once were or cling to the past. Forget yesterday's mistakes.

Never Give Up

At age three, I never gave up finding the pennies Mom threw on the floor as an eye exercise. It was my first lesson that stayed with me throughout life. Mom taught me never to give up, no matter how hard it is. Make it a mindset.

Overcome a Crisis

I overcame a monster in my life—my legal blindness. Most everyone will suffer a traumatic event of some sort in their lifetime. It could be a death, illness, divorce, accident, an attack, or a disaster.

These are some ideas that help in chaotic situations:

- Ask for help if you need it. You'll have a lot of extra things to do in a crisis. Get professional advice— doctors, psychologists, and lawyers—to help get through an event.

- Try to be physically active. Walk, go to a gym, or continue a regular exercise routine. That will help maintain your mental health too.

- Keep doing what you like to do as much as possible. You may not feel like doing things, such as gardening, reading, or meeting friends. But it's vital to be active.

- Eat properly and get enough sleep. Consume plenty of fruits, vegetables, and water. Avoid processed foods and caffeine (late in the day). Don't watch TV or use a computer in the bedroom. Keep the bedroom quiet and dark.

- Offer to help people in a crunch. Invite them to dinner, go on a walk or go for coffee or to a show. Help give them care or suggest someone who can. This could make a tremendous difference in their lives . . . and yours.

- Think carefully about your safety. Drive and walk carefully. Turn off kitchen appliances and irons. Don't risk further calamities.

Grow, Change for the Better

Grow and change for a better you. Don't cling to your yesterday. I thought of changing my permanent residence from Illinois to my condo in Florida for five years. Then I finally did it. I sold my Evanston house, got rid of thirty-six years of belongings and junk, and moved to my Boynton Beach condo permanently. I don't like change, but I'm a different person today and enjoy every minute of each day in my new environment.

Be Who You Want to Be

I wanted to develop my full potential as a visually impaired person, blend in with everyone else, and become a teacher. Many people said that would be impossible. I was stubborn, so I did what I wanted to do. You can distinguish yourself from others by following your dreams and knowing what you want in life. I say:

"I know what I want. I am living the life I was meant to live. I've been guided to find my purpose in life. I'm in control of what happens in my life. I'm living the life I want to live in. Every minute is spent doing what I want to do when I want to do it."

Don't Dwell on Negatives

We all know someone who always complains about something. I think we don't talk as much about the good things in life. Your brain remembers unhappy experiences more than the happy ones. I learned in *Alice in Wonderland* not to dwell on negatives.

I've found some ways to stop thinking about negative things:

- Recognize that you have a challenge to overcome. Accentuate the positive.
- Take your mind off negativity by doing something you love, such as crafts, art, sports, reading, or meeting up with friends.
- Keep busy. Think about how to solve your negativity challenge. If you lost a loved one, don't continually mourn; do something that keeps you active and happy.
- Be confident you'll succeed and move forward. Don't let a small setback throw you off course.

Face Challenges

Face tough challenges that you could fail. Try to accomplish difficult things. When you do, you'll feel so much better. My father made me feel like the family's black sheep. But I removed that emotional stress by going away to college.

Tell Your Life Story

Alice remarked, "There ought to be a book written about me, that there ought! And when I grow up, I'll write one." Everyone has an exciting story to tell, including you. By writing this book, I learned to value my experiences, feelings, and skills. I discovered that this was an essential step towards my own self-fulfillment—doing what I wished to do. And, at ninety-two, I finally found out who I really was in life.

How to Keep a Family Together
(Chapter 7)

I discovered how to survive my family life. Here are some lessons I found on how to keep a family together that may help you:

- Share stories about what happened in each other's day.
- Eat at least one meal a week with all of the family present.
- Do something together as a family once a week, such as watching a movie.
- Make sure children participate in a group activity outside of school and support them in it, such as dance lessons or Little League baseball.
- Create rituals, such as going for pizza on one Friday a month.
- Laugh together often.
- Read stories to each other—from bedtime stories for young children to age-appropriate novels for older children or new articles for adult children.

How to Deal with a Disobedient Child
(Chapter 7)

Child experts say noncompliance or defiance is a good thing. I was trying to be more independent—part of a healthy child's development. But regular disobedience isn't. When Mom loudly called me to come in from playing in the yard, I often pretended not to hear her.

I found several things you can do to motivate kids to start listening better:

- Find behavior to praise. This tells children you appreciate respectful compliance. Create simple requests and praise her for complying, such as asking a child to pass the salt at dinner.

- Give positive attention. Spend time together, talking, or playing a game, for example. This helps prevent much negative attention-seeking using non-compliance.

- Offer two choices. Don't ask questions where a defiant kid will say, "No!" Instead of "Will you get dressed now?" Ask, "Do you want to wear your blue dress or red dress?" She will feel more in control.

- Make sure she hears you. Stop what she is doing. Establish eye contact with her. Don't let her tune you out. Give only the most essential commands.

- Motivate her with a changed message. Encourage compliance and show her she has some control of earning privileges. Instead of saying, "You can't play with your dolls because you haven't cleaned up your room yet." Say, "You can play with your dolls all you want as soon as you're finished cleaning your room."

- Create incentives to be compliant. Give the child a token when she listens and follows your instructions without arguing. She can cash in the tokens for special privileges, such as playing in the park.

Coping with Black Sheep Syndrome (Chapter 8)

How can you stay resilient despite the stress of being a black sheep? Here are my suggestions based on what I did:

1. I focused on loving relationships with my brother and friends. I received support from them.

2. I discovered that I became more durable for my black sheep experience. I decided to complete college as a way to emotionally support myself. I turned something negative into a positive outcome.

3. I moved away from home when I went to college. This created a physical distance—a boundary—from Dad.

4. I tried to reduce the influence family relationships had on my life. I told Dad I wouldn't let him support me any longer and that I would work and then pay to go back to school on my own.

5. I lived the life I wanted to live, despite Dad's disapproval. This was more important to me than fitting into Dad's strictness and perfection mold.

Overcoming a Dysfunctional Family
(Chapter 9)

You can overcome the psychological challenges of a dysfunctional family. It may be difficult and take a lot of patience and work. To build a healthier family, with love, trust, and honesty, you must take responsibility to make the first moves.

Try this: (1) Discuss your feelings with other friendly family members. (2) Learn to trust other people more. (3) Be an example for others in the family by changing yourself. Others may follow you. (4) Talk to friends or professional counselors if you need help.

How to Stop Being Stubborn
(Chapter 14)

Brave people may be called headstrong, obstinate, and unwilling to change. That can be the reason they don't get invited to events, lose friends, and aren't offered jobs. Here are some practical techniques I've found to control persistence:

- Listen to the point of view of the other person, without interrupting them. Look them in the eye. Summarize what they are saying to you.
- Realize that you are not always right. Express your opinion, but others will not always agree with you.

- You may be uncooperative because you don't trust other people. Build trust in them by giving them something simple to do, then harder things.
- Keep an open mind when forming opinions or making judgments.
- Be humble in every situation by being grateful for what you have. Don't inflate yourself. Be modest.
- It's good to be tenacious if you know you are right, are defending something of value, or decide on something that significantly impacts you.

Parenting a Strong-Willed Child (Chapter 14)

Parenting a strong-willed child can be difficult. These kids (and I was one of them) relentlessly go after what they want. They can't bear being told what to do. Don't try to change them because they'll often grow up to be leaders.

Strong-willed kids learn from experience. Let them do that, as long as they don't get hurt. Let them feel in charge of themselves. Don't nag them to do something. Don't say, "Do it because I said so." Instead, listen to your child's point of view, even compromise on different opinions. Ask them a question about what they want to do. Let them have authority over their own bodies.

When I insisted on wearing unlined dress gloves in the subfreezing cold to school, I wish Mom had said to me, "Faith, you are in charge of your own body as long as you stay safe and healthy. I'm going to put your warm mittens

269

in your backpack in case you change your mind." The second I felt my hands freezing, I would have rushed to put on those heavy mittens.

Parents can also set routines and rules to avoid power struggles. Don't force a child to do something. Let him decide himself or on a specific part of it. Treat your child like you would want to be treated. Don't punish a strong will. Let him express his feelings and find a warm relationship with his parents. Give the child respect and empathy.

Understanding a Strong-Willed Spouse (Chapter 14)

I can give you a few tips if you and your spouse or significant other are both strong-willed. This combination can easily lead to power struggles and arguments, as I found out with my husband.

I previously told you strong-willed people learn things from experience. They don't accept what others say. They feel in charge of themselves. When they want something, they push hard for it. Therapists may tell strong-willed wives, "Be more submissive." They might tell strong-willed husbands to be less oppressive.

Here are three essential tips to help resolve conflicts with your strong-willed spouse. (1) Agree to disagree. Winning an argument may not be worth it. Compromise and work at it out without resentment. (2) Create household rules and routines to prevent power struggles. Learn how to compromise graciously. (3) Even if you don't agree, see your spouse's point of view and respect it.

The wills of two strong-willed people are bound to produce disagreements. You can lessen the impact if you understand the other person's strengths and decide to work together to accomplish anything you want.

You Can Change If . . .
(Chapter 14)

It was always hard for me to make changes in my life. You—and everyone—can change for the better. But you must have support from loved ones.

You can change if you:

- Learn from your mistakes. This sounds so simple. But some people make the same mistakes repeatedly. Learn from your mistakes. I did.
- Listen to people. Don't take people for granted. Listen to what they are saying. I certainly didn't because I was obstinate. I wanted to do something my way, not theirs. I heard what they said, but I did it my way. You can communicate better with people if you ask them if what you heard is correct.

How Not to Worry
(Chapter 15)

Here are five simple ways to stop the worrying that causes anxiety, from The Seleni Institute and verified by *Psychology Today*:

- Create positive scenarios for worries that often won't be true. For instance, I could be worried that my daughter didn't call me recently because she was mad at me for something I said (worst-case scenario). My alternate scenario: she was just working hard on a project at work (a more likely scenario).

- Repeat a word or phrase (mantra) anytime to calm your mind. It can be something like "Om" or "Everything will be alright."
- Think about the present, not the past or future, which you can't control.
- Write down your worries to calm a racing, anxious mind. By writing them down on paper or on a computer, you can revisit them later. This will reduce the worries' power and your stress.
- Breathe slowly to lessen stress and worry and find peace. When breathing in, count to three, and when breathing out, count to five. If your mind wanders, concentrate on the breathing.

Don't expect immediate benefits. Practice these steps regularly over an extended period to get results.

Marry Someone You Really Love (Chapter 15)

Romantic love and sex are essential to many people. What have I learned about love and sex that I could pass on to my grandchildren or even adults? When you try to tell the younger generation anything, they generally won't listen. But maybe if I write it . . .

Take your time and make sure you find someone you genuinely love and who will love you back. Don't settle on someone just to get married. Make the right decision for you. Only you know the kind of person who will make you happy. If you experience a feeling and emotion like you never have before, you will know you've found the right person and that you're in love. Don't let the looks or words of the other person fool you into a sense that you are really in love.

Don't let good sex alone determine your marriage or only partner. A long-lasting relationship takes the total commitment of both parties to love each other unconditionally forever. If you pick the wrong partner, learn from your mistake. Don't be miserable, get out of the relationship, and try to find a better one. No one should go through life alone. I hope these suggestions will help you have a full and happy life. You deserve happiness and the joy that I had of being loved.

How to Break Out of Your Comfort Zone (Chapter 17)

Pick something you always wanted to do but are afraid to do it and commit to doing it. You've got to have fun with life. Take chances.

Try these tips to break out of your comfort zone:

1. Try new things that challenge or scare you. It could be something like skydiving or even writing a book.
2. Bring an adventurous friend or family member to try new experiences with you.
3. Research the new adventure on the Internet to know more about it.

4. Commit to the activity or take away a daily activity you love as an incentive.
5. Think positively to overcome fear or fear of failure. It will make you happier and more fulfilled.
6. Just do it!

How to Make Amends
(Chapter 18)

Families can be fantastic—or painful. They can be packed with terrific memories. Or families can be full of hurt, disagreements, and even betrayal. Feuds between siblings are more common than you think. But they can be fixed—in many cases, but not all. Many people want to talk about sibling estrangements and learn how they can forgive.

From my experience, here are some ideas on how to end an estrangement. Say to the person you are estranged from:

- "I want to have a closer relationship with you. I want to end our not speaking for our sake and for the rest of the family." (Tell the positive values of the other person.)
- "What would we each have to do for us to agree to end our separation? (If you agree to that person's request, estrangement ends.) Or . . .
- "I am not opposed to your request, but would you do this (modest) thing for me: Let's agree that we are both to blame, let's not discuss what happened

exactly and let's have a fresh start." (The key point is not to debate, but to talk, give and take, about what each person wants to do.) Or . . .

- "I'm not willing to do what you ask. But I would be willing to do [blank].

- If you reach a breakthrough, tell the person you're so happy to be talking again. Use gentle humor to relieve tension, even making fun of yourself.

- Try to communicate through e-mail or text messages. Don't write a long letter to the other person. Those can be ineffective and misinterpreted. Send a short note, telling how you miss them not being in your life.

- Contact the person who has shut you out every few months for a few years. Don't give up prematurely. Sometimes these things take time. Send a lighthearted note via emails, texts, or letters, whichever seems less intrusive.

ABOUT THE CO-AUTHORS

Dick Robinson is an award-winning journalist, historian, author, speaker, and marketing copywriter. For more  than four decades, he wrote for national newspapers, magazines, journals, and a large public relations firm. The Associated Press and the American Heart Association gave him writing awards, and he was nominated for a Pulitzer Prize. His writing has appeared in *The New York Times, Washington Post* Syndicate, *American Health* and *Health* magazines, and in publications of Burger King, Texaco, Children's Television Workshop, and Capital Cities/ABC. Dick is a professional personal, family, and building historian and president of Legacy Scribe Books, LLC. He dedicates the writing of this book to his late daughter, Kelly Dawn Robinson. Dick welcomes any comments. He may be reached by e-mail at dick@BlindBlackSheep.com.

Faith Brickman Block, 92, legally blind from birth, changed the world. For more than a half-century, she has  taught, motivated, and inspired children with disabilities, seniors with infirmities, and family and friends with difficult life challenges. Born in Chicago, her father Joseph owned a home building company and her mother, Bessie Shear, was a homemaker. Faith had four brothers and one sister. She married the late George Block and they adopted Naomi. A graduate of Roosevelt University, Faith taught disadvantaged elementary students and was the program coordinator for the Council for Jewish Elderly in Evanston, Illinois. Her passions are going to the theater and enjoying every minute of the day.

How did you like *Blind Black Sheep*?

Thank you for reading *Blind Black Sheep*. We're grateful you took this journey with us. We hope you were entertained and found information that helped improve your life. If you enjoyed our book, please share your experience with friends on Facebook and Twitter.

And please give us a review on Amazon. Getting reviews for a book is challenging. A review adds credibility to our publication and helps us tremendously. We would very much appreciate it if you would post a review of our book on Amazon.com. Thank you.

Made in the USA
Columbia, SC
17 June 2020